UNDERSTA

Q The GLORIOUS UR'ĀN

Text, Translation and Commentary

PART *30* WITH
Sūrah al-Fātiḥah

Shaikh-ul-Hind Maulana Maḥmūd Ḥasan
and
'Allama Shabbīr Aḥmad 'Uthmānī

UK ISLAMIC ACADEMY

ISBN 1 872531 40 7 (PB)
ISBN 1 872531 41 5 (HB)

General editor: Iqbal Ahmad Azami

Translation from Urdu: Dr. A.R. Kidwai

Published by

UK Islamic Academy
PO Box 6645
Leicester
LE5 5WT
United Kingdom

British Library Cataloguing-in-Publication Data

A catalogue record for this book is available from the British Library

Design and Typeset by: Muhammad al-Madani

CONTENTS

4

| | An-Nabā' | سُوْرَةُ النَّبَإِ | The Tidings |

| In the name of Allah, Most Compassionate, Most Merciful. |  بِسْمِ اللّٰهِ الرَّحْمٰنِ الرَّحِيْمِ |

1. About what do they ask one another?[1]　عَمَّ يَتَسَآءَلُوْنَ ۟١

2. About the Great Tidings,　عَنِ النَّبَإِ الْعَظِيْمِ ۟٢

3. Regarding which they differ.[2]　الَّذِيْ هُمْ فِيْهِ مُخْتَلِفُوْنَ ۟٣

4. Nay, they will soon come to know,　كَلَّا سَيَعْلَمُوْنَ ۟٤

5. Again nay, they will soon come to know.[3]　ثُمَّ كَلَّا سَيَعْلَمُوْنَ ۟٥

1 – They are asked what it is they are seeking. Are they competent enough to appreciate the Truth they seek? This is not possible. Alternatively, the verse might be taken to mean that the unbelievers questioned themselves about the Day of Judgement about which the Prophet ﷺ informed them. However, they ask him and other Believers when this will be. They insist that it be expedited. These unbelievers are asked to realise the implications of their demand. The Last Day is a great happening and they will soon confront it. Then they will grasp the Truth as they see the dreadful spectacle of the Last Day.

2 – There is much divergence of opinion about the Last Day. Some believe in it whereas others deny it out of hand. Then there are those who doubt it. Still others believe only in bodily Resurrection while others contend that only the soul will be subjected to reward and punishment in the Hereafter. They deny the involvement of the body in this phenomenon. Such differences abound.

3 – Since the first day, God's Messengers have tried hard to reason with mankind. Yet the unbelievers do not give up their questioning

6. Did We not make the earth as a resting place,[4]	أَلَمْ نَجْعَلِ ٱلْأَرْضَ مِهَٰدًا ۝٦
7. And the mountains as pegs?[5]	وَٱلْجِبَالَ أَوْتَادًا ۝٧
8. And We created you in pairs,[6]	وَخَلَقْنَٰكُمْ أَزْوَٰجًا ۝٨
9. And made for you sleep as comfort.[7]	وَجَعَلْنَا نَوْمَكُمْ سُبَاتًا ۝٩
10. And We made the night as a cover,[8]	وَجَعَلْنَا ٱلَّيْلَ لِبَاسًا ۝١٠
11. And made the day as a means of sustenance.[9]	وَجَعَلْنَا ٱلنَّهَارَ مَعَاشًا ۝١١

and doubt. Soon they will be faced with the Dreadful Day. Only then will they realise what the Day of Judgement is and that their questionings and doubts were without any basis.

4 – In other words, the land on which man rests and sleeps.

5 – Once something is tied firmly, it cannot be shaken. Initially, the earth was in a state of constant trembling. Allah created the mountains which put an end to this. The earth thus gained constancy and tranquillity, thanks to the placement of mountains on it.

6 – Allah has blessed man with a female spouse for his comfort and relief. A verse of similar import is *Sūrah ar-Rūm*: 21. Alternatively, the reference may be to the variety of spouses in terms of their complexion and colour.

7 – After a hard day one sleeps, such that one is totally refreshed when one gets up the next day. Sleep is synonymous with comfort. This is followed by an account of the night.

8 – As clothes cover the body, the darkness of the night envelops everyone. Generally speaking, secret acts are done in the darkness of the night. One needs thicker clothes at night as it is colder then.

9 – Generally speaking, one earns one's bread in daylight. This gives one the opportunity to meet the needs of one's family. This account

12. And We built above you seven strong firmaments,[10]	وَبَنَيْنَا فَوْقَكُمْ سَبْعًا شِدَادًا ۝
13. And placed a bright lamp (therein).[11]	وَجَعَلْنَا سِرَاجًا وَهَّاجًا ۝
14. And We sent down from the clouds heavy rain,[12]	وَأَنزَلْنَا مِنَ ٱلْمُعْصِرَٰتِ مَآءً ثَجَّاجًا ۝
15. So that We may produce thereby corn and vegetation,	لِّنُخْرِجَ بِهِۦ حَبًّا وَنَبَاتًا ۝
16. And gardens full of luxurious growth.[13]	وَجَنَّٰتٍ أَلْفَافًا ۝
17. Indeed the Day of Judgement is an appointed time,[14]	إِنَّ يَوْمَ ٱلْفَصْلِ كَانَ مِيقَٰتًا ۝

of day and night is followed by that of the heavens and the earth. In other words, the earth is contrasted with the sky in the following passage.

10 – Allah has created seven firm spheres of the heavens. Notwithstanding the passage of such a long period of time, no gap has ever marred the sky.

11 – That is the sun which stands out both for its heat and its light.

12 – Reference is made here to the rain-laden clouds.

13 – That is thick forests. Alternatively, the point made is that Allah has created a wide range of trees and orchards. This account of the outstanding Signs of Divine Power is followed by the conclusion that since Allah is All-Powerful and All-Wise, it is not at all hard for Him to resurrect mankind and subject him to the Reckoning. For, it runs contrary to His Wisdom that the universe would come to an end without any accountability. Reason demands that there should be a logical end to the present order, and this is known in Qur'ānic terminology as the Hereafter. As one wakes up after sleep and night follows day, this world is to be followed by the Hereafter. This is certain, beyond any shadow of a doubt.

14 – On the Day of Judgement, the pious will stand apart from the wicked. There will not be any intermixing of good and evil on that Day.

18. The Day the trumpet will be blown,	يَوْمَ يُنفَخُ فِى ٱلصُّورِ
Then you will rush forth in multitudes,15	فَتَأْتُونَ أَفْوَاجًا ﴿١٨﴾
19. And the sky will be opened and it will have gates,16	وَفُتِحَتِ ٱلسَّمَآءُ فَكَانَتْ أَبْوَٰبًا ﴿١٩﴾
20. And the mountains will be removed	وَسُيِّرَتِ ٱلْجِبَالُ
And reduced to shining sand.17	فَكَانَتْ سَرَابًا ﴿٢٠﴾
21. Indeed Hell lies in ambush.	إِنَّ جَهَنَّمَ كَانَتْ مِرْصَادًا ﴿٢١﴾
22. It is the abode for the wicked.18	لِّلطَّٰغِينَ مَـَٔابًا ﴿٢٢﴾

Everyone will reach his ultimate destination. Perfect recompense is not attainable in this life. For numerous things are equally enjoyed by both Believers and unbelievers in this life, as for example, the sun, the moon, the earth, the sky, night and day, sleeping and waking, rain and clouds, fields and farms and wives and children. It is, therefore, imperative that the Day of Judgement be at the end of the present order. Its exact Day is known to Allah alone.

15 – Reference is made here to the numerous groups who will emerge in relation to their deeds and Faith.

16 – The sky will be so badly rent asunder as if it had gaps at every point. Almost the same idea is presented in verse 25 of *Sūrah al-Furqān*.

17 – The reference here is to a mirage. Likewise, one will mistake them as mountains, though these too will have been reduced to sand dunes.

18 – Hell lies in ambush for the wicked and will serve as their Eternal Abode.

23. They will abide therein for ages.[19]

لَّبِثِينَ فِيهَآ أَحۡقَابًا ﴿٢٣﴾

24. They will not taste therein any coolness,

لَّا يَذُوقُونَ فِيهَا بَرۡدًا

Nor will they have any drink,

وَلَا شَرَابًا ﴿٢٤﴾

25. Except boiling water and pus.[20]

إِلَّا حَمِيمًا وَغَسَّاقًا ﴿٢٥﴾

26. It is a fitting recompense.

جَزَآءً وِفَاقًا ﴿٢٦﴾

27. They did not expect the Reckoning,

إِنَّهُمۡ كَانُواْ لَا يَرۡجُونَ حِسَابًا ﴿٢٧﴾

28. Rather they rejected Our Signs totally as false.[21]

وَكَذَّبُواْ بِـَٔايَٰتِنَا كِذَّابًا ﴿٢٨﴾

29. And We have preserved everything on record.[22]

وَكُلَّ شَيۡءٍ أَحۡصَيۡنَٰهُ كِتَٰبًا ﴿٢٩﴾

19 – Time, in the context of the Hereafter, is immeasurable. Centuries will pass and still the unbelievers' plight will not end.

20 – The wicked will not enjoy anything good there. They will not be blessed with coolness or any pleasant drink. Rather, boiling water will be served to them which will scald their mouths and intestines. Moreover, they will be offered the pus which flows from their own wounds. May Allah protect us against all forms of punishment in both worlds. *Āmeen.*

21 – What they disregarded altogether will stare them in the face. What they belied will appear there as an undeniable reality. It will then be impossible to reject it any longer.

22 – Allah embraces everything in His knowledge and the same is already recorded. Nothing good or evil happens without His knowledge. Everyone will be recompensed in full for each and every act.

30. Now taste (the fruits of your deeds).	فَذُوقُوا
We shall give you no increase except in punishment.[23]	فَلَن نَّزِيدَكُمْ إِلَّا عَذَابًا ۝
31. Indeed the pious will attain their objective.	إِنَّ لِلْمُتَّقِينَ مَفَازًا ۝
32. Gardens enclosed and vineyards,	حَدَآئِقَ وَأَعْنَٰبًا ۝
33. And young maidens of the same age,[24]	وَكَوَاعِبَ أَتْرَابًا ۝
34. And an overflowing cup.[25]	وَكَأْسًا دِهَاقًا ۝
35. They will not hear therein any vanity or falsehood.[26]	لَّا يَسْمَعُونَ فِيهَا لَغْوًا وَلَا كِذَّٰبًا ۝
36. Recompense from your Lord, in perfect measure.[27]	جَزَآءً مِّن رَّبِّكَ عَطَآءً حِسَابًا ۝

23 – The unbelievers will be told that they exceeded all the limits in their unbelief and rejection of the Truth. Had they not been overwhelmed by death, they would have grown further in their wickedness. They will be made to taste the punishment of their unbelief. Their punishment will be increased in relation to the degree of their unbelief. Their punishment will never be lightened.

24 – Young women in the prime of their youth and they will be of equal age.

25 – That is cups of pure drink.

26 – There will be no vain talk in Paradise. Nor will there be any deception or falsehood. Its occupants will not quarrel with one another. As a result, no one will ever resort to falsehood or deception.

27 – There will be a full recompense for everything and everyone will be treated with perfect justice.

37. The Lord of the heavens and earth	رَبِّ ٱلسَّمَوَٰتِ وَٱلْأَرْضِ
And all that is between these. He is Most Compassionate.[28]	وَمَا بَيْنَهُمَا ٱلرَّحْمَٰنِ
It is not possible for any to demand an audience with Him.[29]	لَا يَمْلِكُونَ مِنْهُ خِطَابًا ۝
38. The Day the spirit and the angels will stand in rows,[30]	يَوْمَ يَقُومُ ٱلرُّوحُ وَٱلْمَلَٰٓئِكَةُ صَفًّا
And none will be able to speak except (he) who	لَّا يَتَكَلَّمُونَ إِلَّا مَنْ
Is granted permission by the Most Compassionate	أَذِنَ لَهُ ٱلرَّحْمَٰنُ
And who speaks the Truth.[31]	وَقَالَ صَوَابًا ۝

28 – The reward will represent Divine Forgiveness and Mercy. As it is, Allah does not owe anything to anyone. It is hard for man to avoid Hellfire on the basis of his deeds alone. One enters Paradise, thanks only to Allah's Grace and Mercy. That Allah describes it as a reward shows His appreciation of man's efforts. Praise be to our Lord.

29 – Notwithstanding His tremendous affection and Mercy, He is so Glorious and Mighty that no one dare move his lips in His presence.

30 – The reference here is to living beings or the Holy Spirit, Gabriel. And according to some commentators the spirit means that mighty spirit from where countless spirits have emanated. Allah knows best.

31 – Only those granted leave will speak in His presence. Furthermore, their utterances will be characterised by reason and Truth. They will not intercede on behalf of those who do not deserve it. Only such are entitled to intercession who embraced the credal statement of Islam – "There is no god except Allah."

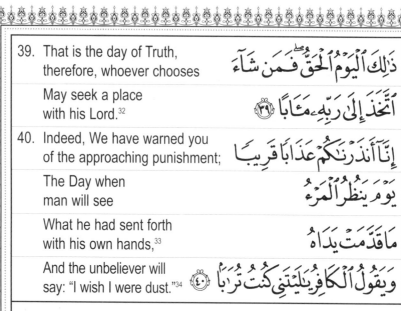

39. That is the day of Truth, therefore, whoever chooses	ذَٰلِكَ ٱلۡيَوۡمُ ٱلۡحَقُّ فَمَن شَآءَ
May seek a place with his Lord.[32]	ٱتَّخَذَ إِلَىٰ رَبِّهِۦ مَـَٔابًا ۝
40. Indeed, We have warned you of the approaching punishment;	إِنَّآ أَنذَرۡنَٰكُمۡ عَذَابًا قَرِيبًا
The Day when man will see	يَوۡمَ يَنظُرُ ٱلۡمَرۡءُ
What he had sent forth with his own hands,[33]	مَا قَدَّمَتۡ يَدَاهُ
And the unbeliever will say: "I wish I were dust."[34]	وَيَقُولُ ٱلۡكَافِرُ يَٰلَيۡتَنِى كُنتُ تُرَٰبَۢا ۝

32 – The Day of Judgement is inevitable. Whoever seeks success should make preparations for that Day.

33 – A record of all deeds, both past and present, will be presented before each person.

34 – The unbelievers will wish that they had been consigned forever to dust. Or that they had not been born as human beings in that it would have saved them their trial on the Day of Judgement.

* * *

| An-Nāzi'āt | سُوْرَةُ النَّازِعَاتِ | Those Who Drag Forth |

In the name of Allah, Most Compassionate, Most Merciful.

1. By the (angels) who take out (the unbelievers' souls) with a vehement pulling.[1]

وَالنَّازِعَاتِ غَرْقًا ۝

2. By those who gently release[2] (the Believers' souls)

وَالنَّاشِطَاتِ نَشْطًا ۝

3. And those who glide fast.

وَالسَّابِحَاتِ سَبْحًا ۝

4. Then those who race with a fast speed.[3]

فَالسَّابِقَاتِ سَبْقًا ۝

5. And who then manage the commands of their Lord.[4]

فَالْمُدَبِّرَاتِ أَمْرًا ۝

1 – The oath refers to the angels who enter into the veins of disbelievers in order to drag their souls out violently.

2 – Reference is made here to those angels who liberate the souls of true Believers; the latter rush to their Lord like a person released from confinement. Note though, that the reference is to the soul and not to the body. The pious welcome the return to their Lord whereas the wicked hate it. The latter are dragged to their evil destination.

3 – Those angels who swiftly carry the souls to the heavens. They float so easily as one swims in water. Furthermore, they instantly implement the Divine directive about each soul.

4 – These angels make the necessary arrangements about every soul, whether it is to be punished or rewarded. Alternatively, the reference might be to the angels who in a general sense look after the working of this universe. The Qur'ānic expressions *an-Nazi'āt* and *an-Nāshiṭāt* have been interpreted variously. Our commentary is in line with the translator's preference.

6.	The Day of Trembling.[5]	يَوْمَ تَرْجُفُ ٱلرَّاجِفَةُ ۝
7.	It will be followed by another (blast).[6]	تَتْبَعُهَا ٱلرَّادِفَةُ ۝
8.	Hearts will throb that Day.	قُلُوبٌ يَوْمَئِذٍ وَاجِفَةٌ ۝
9.	Their eyes will be downcast.[7]	أَبْصَـٰرُهَا خَـٰشِعَةٌ ۝
10.	They say: "Will we be restored to our former state	يَقُولُونَ أَءِنَّا لَمَرْدُودُونَ فِى ٱلْحَافِرَةِ ۝
11.	After we have been reduced to dry bones?"	أَءِذَا كُنَّا عِظَـٰمًا نَّخِرَةً ۝
12.	They say: "This Resurrection is indeed a loss."[8]	قَالُوا تِلْكَ إِذًا كَرَّةٌ خَاسِرَةٌ ۝
13.	So it is a single cry.	فَإِنَّمَا هِىَ زَجْرَةٌ وَٰحِدَةٌ ۝

5 – The earth will be shaken by an earthquake when the trumpet is blown for the first time.

6 – Shāh 'Abdul Qādir Dehlawī remarks (in *Mūḍiḥ al-Qur'ān*): "There will be a series of earthquakes." However, other Qur'ānic scholars explain *ar-Rādifa* in terms of the second blowing of the trumpet. Allah knows best.

7 – Their hearts will pound with panic and distress. Likewise, their eyes will be downcast owing to their humiliation and embarrassment.

8 – They say that it is impossible that they will be Resurrected. For them, it is unthinkable that disintegrated bones will be brought back to life. This will indeed be a major loss for them. For they have made no preparation for the Hereafter. They ridicule Islamic doctrine, firmly believing that there is no Life-after-Death. They are, therefore, indifferent to any loss or gain on this count.

14. Then they all will appear on a vast plain.[9]

فَإِذَا هُم بِالسَّاهِرَةِ ﴿١٤﴾

15. Did the account of Moses reach you?[10]

هَلْ أَتَىٰكَ حَدِيثُ مُوسَىٰٓ ﴿١٥﴾

16. When his Lord called him

إِذْ نَادَىٰهُ رَبُّهُۥ

In the sacred valley of Ṭuwā.[11]

بِالْوَادِ الْمُقَدَّسِ طُوًى ﴿١٦﴾

17. "Go forth towards Pharaoh who has indeed rebelled."

اذْهَبْ إِلَىٰ فِرْعَوْنَ إِنَّهُۥ طَغَىٰ ﴿١٧﴾

18. So say, "It is better for you if you purify yourself.

فَقُلْ هَل لَّكَ إِلَىٰٓ أَن تَزَكَّىٰ ﴿١٨﴾

19. I will guide you to your Lord, so you should fear."[12]

وَأَهْدِيَكَ إِلَىٰ رَبِّكَ فَتَخْشَىٰ ﴿١٩﴾

9 – The unbelievers regard Resurrection as something impossible. However, Allah will accomplish it within no time. As soon as Allah directs that the trumpet be blown, all the dead will instantly appear in the Grand Assembly. Reference is made here to the Divine rebuke. An illustration of this is also provided, which relates to an arrogant person. These unbelievers are told about the humiliating end of earlier unbelievers.

10 – This story has been discussed at length at other places of the Qur'ān.

11 – That is near Mount Ṭūr.

12 – The Prophet Moses عليه السلام told Pharaoh that he could help the latter by Allah's leave and guide him to the way which would infuse in his heart fear of Allah and His gnosis. Without fear of Allah, one cannot grasp the higher Truth. One thus learns that one of the objectives of the Prophet Moses عليه السلام was to reform Pharaoh. His mission did not only consist in liberating the Children of Israel.

20. Then he showed him the Great Sign.[13]	فَأَرَىٰهُ ٱلْأَيَةَ ٱلْكُبْرَىٰ ﴿٢٠﴾
21. Yet he rejected it as false and rebelled.	فَكَذَّبَ وَعَصَىٰ ﴿٢١﴾
22. Then he turned away, striving (against Allah).[14]	ثُمَّ أَدْبَرَ يَسْعَىٰ ﴿٢٢﴾
23. So he gathered his people and called out.	فَحَشَرَ فَنَادَىٰ ﴿٢٣﴾
24. And he said: "I am your Lord, most high."[15]	فَقَالَ أَنَا۠ رَبُّكُمُ ٱلْأَعْلَىٰ ﴿٢٤﴾
25. Then Allah seized him with	فَأَخَذَهُ ٱللَّهُ
The punishment in the Hereafter and in this life.[16]	نَكَالَ ٱلْأَخِرَةِ وَٱلْأُولَىٰ ﴿٢٥﴾
26. Indeed, in this is the lesson for the one who fears.[17]	إِنَّ فِى ذَٰلِكَ لَعِبْرَةً لِّمَن يَخْشَىٰ ﴿٢٦﴾

13 – On approaching Pharaoh, the Prophet Moses عليه السلام conveyed to him the Divine Message, and in order to clinch the argument he presented before him the great miracle of the rod turning into a serpent.

14 – Pharaoh, being an accursed person, refused altogether to believe. He thought of assembling the public and summoned his magicians in order to counter the Prophet Moses عليه السلام.

15 – Pharaoh considered himself as the supreme lord. He, therefore, rejected the Prophet's claim to Messengership.

16 – Pharaoh was drowned. In the Next Life he will be roasted in Hellfire.

17 – There are many lessons in this story, provided the reader has some fear of Allah. The story of the Prophet Moses عليه السلام and Pharaoh is followed by a resumption of the main subject matter, the Hereafter.

27. What is more difficult, your creation	ءَأَنتُمْ أَشَدُّ خَلْقًا
Or that of the heavens?[18] He has created both.	أَمِ السَّمَآءُ بَنَىٰهَا ۝ 
28. He raised it and levelled it.	رَفَعَ سَمْكَهَا فَسَوَّىٰهَا ۝ 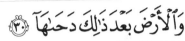
29. And He made the night dark and brought forth the dawn.[19]	وَأَغْطَشَ لَيْلَهَا وَأَخْرَجَ ضُحَىٰهَا ۝ 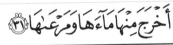
30. And after this He laid out the earth.[20]	وَالْأَرْضَ بَعْدَ ذَٰلِكَ دَحَىٰهَا ۝
31. He brought forth from it its water and its produce.[21]	أَخْرَجَ مِنْهَا مَآءَهَا وَمَرْعَىٰهَا ۝

18 – The creation of mankind is no more difficult than the creation of other objects of the universe such as the sky, the earth and mountains. Since man looks upon Allah as the Creator of these objects, he should not have any reservations about Allah's ability to Resurrect them.

19 – Attention is drawn to the sky. It appears as very lofty, firm, clear, smooth and well-organised. Then Allah has devised a perfect working of the movement of the sun and the alternation of day and night. The sky has a different appearance at night and looks totally different in the sunlight.

20 – As to who was created prior to the creation of the heavens and the earth, this point has been addressed by us at an earlier place in our commentary on *Sūrah Fuṣṣilat*. The Qur'ānic expression *Daḥā* is defined by Imām Rāghib (in *Mufradāt al-Qur'ān*) as replacing something after having fixed it at a particular place. Taken in this sense, it may be reconciled to modern theories about the birth of the planet earth, which was initially part of a larger planetary system. And Allah knows best.

21 – Allah made the rivers and springs to flow. Then He created greenery out of water.

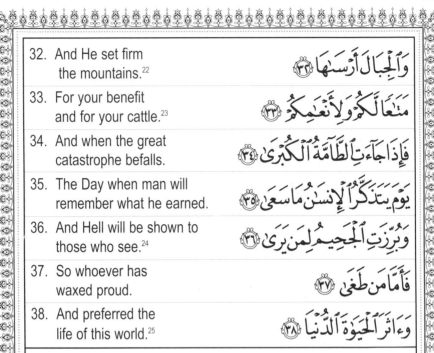

32. And He set firm the mountains.[22]

وَٱلْجِبَالَ أَرْسَىٰهَا ﴿٣٢﴾

33. For your benefit and for your cattle.[23]

مَتَٰعًا لَّكُمْ وَلِأَنْعَٰمِكُمْ ﴿٣٣﴾

34. And when the great catastrophe befalls.

فَإِذَا جَآءَتِ ٱلطَّآمَّةُ ٱلْكُبْرَىٰ ﴿٣٤﴾

35. The Day when man will remember what he earned.

يَوْمَ يَتَذَكَّرُ ٱلْإِنسَٰنُ مَا سَعَىٰ ﴿٣٥﴾

36. And Hell will be shown to those who see.[24]

وَبُرِّزَتِ ٱلْجَحِيمُ لِمَن يَرَىٰ ﴿٣٦﴾

37. So whoever has waxed proud.

فَأَمَّا مَن طَغَىٰ ﴿٣٧﴾

38. And preferred the life of this world.[25]

وَءَاثَرَ ٱلْحَيَوٰةَ ٱلدُّنْيَا ﴿٣٨﴾

22 – Reference is to the unshakeable mountains. They keep the earth steady in the face of earthquakes.

23 – In the absence of this perfect arrangement, men and animals would not have survived. Allah has created everything so as to cater for and comfort man. It is, therefore, obligatory on man to constantly thank his true Benefactor. Since Allah is All-Powerful and All-Wise and has put in place such an amazing arrangement for man's existence, it is not hard at all for Him to Resurrect man. Man must acknowledge Divine Power and Glory and devote himself to thanking Him for His numerous favours. Otherwise, man will regret and be full of remorse on the Day of Judgement when he will confront his record of deeds.

24 – Hell will be presented before them in a manner that everyone sees it. All barriers will be removed.

25 – The unbelievers preferred this life to the Hereafter and opted for the former, mistaking it as better.

39. His abode will be Hell.

فَإِنَّ ٱلْجَحِيمَ هِىَ ٱلْمَأْوَىٰ ﴿٣٩﴾

40. And whoever stands full
of fear before his Lord

وَأَمَّا مَنْ خَافَ مَقَامَ رَبِّهِۦ

And restrains the self
from base desires.

وَنَهَى ٱلنَّفْسَ عَنِ ٱلْهَوَىٰ ﴿٤٠﴾

41. His abode is the Garden.[26]

فَإِنَّ ٱلْجَنَّةَ هِىَ ٱلْمَأْوَىٰ ﴿٤١﴾

42. They ask you:
"When will be the Hour?"[27]

يَسْـَٔلُونَكَ عَنِ ٱلسَّاعَةِ أَيَّانَ مُرْسَىٰهَا ﴿٤٢﴾

43. Its account
does not concern you.

فِيمَ أَنتَ مِن ذِكْرَىٰهَآ ﴿٤٣﴾

44. Its knowledge
is with your Lord.[28]

إِلَىٰ رَبِّكَ مُنتَهَىٰهَآ ﴿٤٤﴾

45. You are the warner
for those who fear it.[29]

إِنَّمَآ أَنتَ مُنذِرُ مَن يَخْشَىٰهَا ﴿٤٥﴾

26 – Reference is made to the Believers who were ever conscious of their appearance one day before Allah. Accordingly, they are not dictated to by the desires of their own selves. Rather, they control themselves and surrender themselves to the Divine Will. Such are destined to enter Paradise.

27 – The unbelievers repeatedly ask when the Day of Judgement will be.

28 – The Prophet ﷺ cannot identify the exact time and date of the Day of Judgement. Its knowledge rests only with Allah, no matter what questions and doubts the unbelievers put. Shāh ʿAbdul Qādir comments: "The unbelievers might keep on raising these questions. However, they have to appear ultimately before Allah. Everyone is unaware of its exact day of happening."

29 – The Prophet's mission consists in warning people against the Day of Judgement. Whoever is concerned about his ultimate end

46. On that Day will feel as if they had stayed in the world

كَأَنَّهُمْ يَوْمَ يَرَوْنَهَا لَمْ يَلْبَثُوٓا

Except for a morning or an evening.[30]

إِلَّا عَشِيَّةً أَوْ ضُحَىٰهَا ﴿٤٦﴾

will get the point and make preparations for the Last Day. His warning is, therefore, helpful only for those who are inclined to the Truth. As for unbelievers, they are disregardful of their ultimate end and waste their time and energy in such peripheral issues as the day and date of this happening.

30 – The unbelievers asked that the Day of Judgement be expedited. However, when it overwhelms them, they will feel that it has overtaken them too soon and too suddenly. They will feel that it did not take long for the Last Day to befall them.

* * *

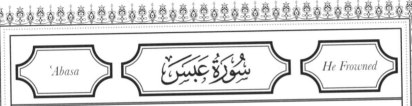

'Abasa	He Frowned

In the name of Allah, Most Compassionate, Most Merciful.

1. He frowned[1] and turned away

2. A blind person who approached him.[2]

1 – The Prophet ﷺ was instructing the Quraysh chiefs in the fundamentals of Islam. Meanwhile a blind Muslim, Ibn Umm Maktūm, visited him and sought his attention. He had a query about a Qur'ānic verse and requested to know its meaning and message. He said: "O Messenger of Allah! Teach me out of what Allah has taught you." The Prophet ﷺ was not happy with this interruption, thinking that he was engaged in a much more important task. For if the Quraysh chiefs embraced Islam, a large number of people would follow them in accepting Islam. On the other hand, Ibn Umm Maktūm was already a Muslim who could learn finer details of Faith at any time. He could not have realised that the Prophet ﷺ was pre-occupied with the influential members of society. Were they guided, it could result in the guidance of thousands of others. The Prophet ﷺ, therefore, disapproved of the interruption. He knew also that if he disregarded the Quraysh chiefs in order to satisfy Ibn Umm Maktūm's query, they would feel offended. They would probably walk away. In sum, the Prophet ﷺ was displeased and this reflected on his face. It was against this background that these verses were revealed. According to authentic reports, whenever Ibn Umm Maktūm visited the Prophet ﷺ in the future, he was received very warmly, saying: "Welcome! It was for you that my Lord chided me."

2 – The Prophet ﷺ turned his face as the blind person approached him. He should, however, have paid greater attention to him in

3. And what do you know?
Maybe he would have been purified. ﴿٣﴾   وَمَا يُدْرِيكَ لَعَلَّهُۥ يَزَّكَّىٰٓ

4. Or he would have
been admonished.   أَوْ يَذَّكَّرُ

And the admonition
would have benefited him.[3]   فَتَنفَعَهُ ٱلذِّكْرَىٰٓ ﴿٤﴾

5. As to him who regards
himself self-sufficient.   أَمَّا مَنِ ٱسْتَغْنَىٰ ﴿٥﴾

6. You are concerned about him,   فَأَنتَ لَهُۥ تَصَدَّىٰ ﴿٦﴾

7. There is no blame upon you
if he does not mend his ways.[4]   وَمَا عَلَيْكَ أَلَّا يَزَّكَّىٰ ﴿٧﴾

view of his disability and his quest for the Truth. Shāh 'Abdul Qādir states: "This account relates to the Prophet ﷺ. It is followed by a direct address to him." Other scholars opine that the Prophet ﷺ is not addressed directly in these verses out of regard for him. Rather, he is addressed indirectly later lest he might feel Allah's indifference towards him. And Allah knows best.

3 – That blind companion was a genuine seeker of the Truth. The Prophet's attention could have improved his lot and purified his soul. Or he could have reflected sincerely upon the Prophet's teachings and this would have helped him at a later stage.

4 – Those who disregard the Truth out of pride and arrogance find it hard to surrender themselves to Allah and His Messenger. The Prophet ﷺ is, however, very keen on their acceptance of Faith, thinking that their conversion will inspire others as well. Allah will not hold the Prophet ﷺ responsible for the refusal and failure of arrogant people to respond to him. His mission is to convey the Truth, which he has performed well. He need not focus his attention too much on their acceptance of Faith and at the expense of neglecting genuine seekers of Truth and true Believers. Commoners could have misinterpreted this incident seeing in it that the Prophet ﷺ was more

8. However, one who called on you, rushing.	وَأَمَّا مَن جَآءَكَ يَسْعَىٰ ۝
9. He fears.[5]	وَهُوَ يَخْشَىٰ ۝
10. However, you are indifferent to him.[6]	فَأَنتَ عَنْهُ تَلَهَّىٰ ۝
11. Nay, this is the admonition.	كَلَّآ إِنَّهَا تَذْكِرَةٌ ۝
12. Whoever wills may recite it.[7]	فَمَن شَآءَ ذَكَرَهُۥ ۝
13. It is in the honourable scrolls.	فِى صُحُفٍ مُّكَرَّمَةٍ ۝

particular about the wealthy and influential members of society and so displayed an indifference. Such a misunderstanding could damage the cause of Islam. The advantage accruing from the acceptance of Islam by these chiefs was less than any possible damage to the cause of Islam.

5 – Ibn Umm Maktūm feared Allah and always looked forward to visiting the Prophet ﷺ. Being blind he did not have an escort to take him to the Prophet ﷺ. He could stumble on the way, or the unbelievers could persecute him, in the sure knowledge that he was on his way to meet the Prophet ﷺ.

6 – Only genuine seekers of Truth are likely to believe and help the cause of Islam. It is reported that Ibn Umm Maktūm participated actively in the Battle of Qādsiyah while clad in his coat of arms. He attained martyrdom in the same Battle. May Allah be pleased with him.

7 – If arrogant, wealthy unbelievers do not recite the Qur'ān and pay no heed to its teachings, they will incur self-destruction. Nor should the Prophet ﷺ feel too much concern on their account. A general note of advice is made here. Whoever is interested in his own welfare should recite and follow the Qur'ān.

14. Elevated and purified.[8]	مَّرْفُوعَةٍ مُّطَهَّرَةٍ ۝
15. By the hands of scribes.	بِأَيْدِى سَفَرَةٍ ۝
16. They are of high rank and righteous.[9]	كِرَامٍ بَرَرَةٍ ۝
17. Perish man! How ungrateful he is![10]	قُتِلَ ٱلْإِنسَٰنُ مَآ أَكْفَرَهُۥ ۝
18. From what is he created?	مِنْ أَىِّ شَىْءٍ خَلَقَهُۥ ۝
19. From a drop.[11] He created him and proportioned him.[12]	مِن نُّطْفَةٍ خَلَقَهُۥ فَقَدَّرَهُۥ ۝

8 – The Qur'ān is not likely to benefit from the Faith of those arrogant chiefs. The Qur'ānic verses are recorded in exalted pages in the heavens. True Believers on earth also pay extreme regard to the pages of the Qur'ān and maintain its purity.

9 – The angels record the Qur'ān and Divine Revelation is sent down to the Prophet ﷺ. Likewise, on earth, the most virtuous Believers are engaged in recording and compiling the Qur'ān. They are absolutely free from any thought of tampering with its text.

10 – The unbelievers are guilty of disregarding such a major bounty as the Qur'ān. Nor do they discharge the obligations which they owe to Allah.

11 – With a little reflection, the unbelievers will have realised their lowly origin. They were created out of a mere drop of water, devoid of any sense-perception, beauty and understanding. It is Allah Who blesses man with all these at a later stage. Since man originates from lowly origins, it does not become him to argue with his Creator and Benefactor and disregard His Guidance. Man should feel deeply embarrassed at treating his Master and Benefactor so ungratefully.

12 – Allah has created and proportioned all limbs in certain measure. No creation is without an underlying purpose and wisdom.

20. Then He made the path easy for him.[13]	ثُمَّ ٱلسَّبِيلَ يَسَّرَهُۥ ﴿٢٠﴾
21. Then He caused his death and got him placed in the grave.[14]	ثُمَّ أَمَاتَهُۥ فَأَقْبَرَهُۥ ﴿٢١﴾
22. And whenever He Wills, He will resurrect him.[15]	ثُمَّ إِذَا شَآءَ أَنشَرَهُۥ ﴿٢٢﴾
23. Nay, he has not yet fulfilled what Allah commanded him.[16]	كَلَّا لَمَّا يَقْضِ مَآ أَمَرَهُۥ ﴿٢٣﴾
24. Let man look at his food.[17]	فَلْيَنظُرِ ٱلْإِنسَٰنُ إِلَىٰ طَعَامِهِۦٓ ﴿٢٤﴾
25. We make the rains fall from above.	أَنَّا صَبَبْنَا ٱلْمَآءَ صَبًّا ﴿٢٥﴾

13 – Allah enables man to distinguish between Faith and unbelief. Or it might stand for easy delivery from the mother's womb.

14 – Allah has directed that man be buried after his death. This protects against any disfiguring of one's body after death.

15 – It is Allah Who causes life and death. He Alone exercises the authority to resurrect whoever when it pleases Him. No one can withhold Him. Since Allah alone has authority over such matters as causing one's birth, transporting one to *Barzakh* and resurrecting one in the Grand Assembly, it does not befit anyone to defy Him, disregard His Guidance or forget His numerous favours.

16 – Man fails to appreciate Allah's Glory and Greatness and does not perform the duty assigned to him. Ibn Kathīr reads verse 22 in conjunction with verse 23 of this *Sūrah*. Allah is free to resurrect man as and when He Wills. Resurrection is not possible at this stage. For His earlier decree about a certain figure for the human population has not reached its mark.

17 – After describing man's origin and death, the provision for his life and existence is now related.

26. Then We make the earth split.[18]	ثُمَّ شَقَقْنَا ٱلْأَرْضَ شَقًّا ۝
27. Then We cause the corn to grow in it.	فَأَنۢبَتۡنَا فِيهَا حَبًّا ۝
28. And grapes and vegetables.	وَعِنَبًا وَقَضۡبًا ۝
29. And olives and datepalms.	وَزَيۡتُونًا وَنَخۡلًا ۝
30. And enclosed gardens.	وَحَدَآئِقَ غُلۡبًا ۝
31. And fruits and herbage.	وَفَٰكِهَةً وَأَبًّا ۝
32. For your benefit and for your cattle.[19]	مَّتَٰعًا لَّكُمۡ وَلِأَنۡعَٰمِكُمۡ ۝
33. And when it befalls which will blast the ear.[20]	فَإِذَا جَآءَتِ ٱلصَّآخَّةُ ۝
34. The Day one will flee from his brother.	يَوۡمَ يَفِرُّ ٱلۡمَرۡءُ مِنۡ أَخِيهِ ۝
35. From his mother and his father.	وَأُمِّهِۦ وَأَبِيهِ ۝
36. And from his wife and sons.	وَصَٰحِبَتِهِۦ وَبَنِيهِ ۝

18 – Even a single blade of grass cannot grow on its own. It is Allah Who helps man obtain a large variety of grain, fruits, vegetables and other products from the soil.

19 – Some of these products are consumed by man and others by cattle.

20 – Its sound will be so intense that it would render everyone deaf. The obvious reference here is to the blowing of the trumpet.

37. For everyone that Day

There will be a concern
which will overwhelm him.[21]

لِكُلِّ ٱمْرِيٍٕ مِّنْهُمْ يَوْمَئِذٍ شَأْنٌ يُغْنِيهِ ۝

38. Many faces that Day
will be bright.

وُجُوهٌ يَوْمَئِذٍ مُّسْفِرَةٌ ۝

39. Laughing and rejoicing.[22]

ضَاحِكَةٌ مُّسْتَبْشِرَةٌ ۝

40. And many faces that Day
will be stained with dust.

وَوُجُوهٌ يَوْمَئِذٍ عَلَيْهَا غَبَرَةٌ ۝

41. Blackness will cover them.[23]

تَرْهَقُهَا قَتَرَةٌ ۝

42. They are the ones who
disbelieved and persisted.[24]

أُوْلَٰئِكَ هُمُ ٱلْكَفَرَةُ ٱلْفَجَرَةُ ۝

21 – Everyone will be full of worry on his own account on the Day of Judgement. Friends and close relatives will not enquire after one another's welfare lest others may ask for the loan of good deeds. Therefore everyone will flee from everyone else.

22 – The faces of true Believers will be radiant with the light of Faith and ecstasy.

23 – The ugliness of unbelief will disfigure the unbelievers' faces. Furthermore, their faces will be darkened with their wickedness. As a result, they will appear all the darker and repulsive.

24 – The unbelievers are so brazen that they do not take any heed, no matter how much they are instructed in Truth. Nor do they fear Allah or feel embarrassment towards their fellow creatures.

***

| At-Takwīr | سُورَةُ التَّكْوِيرِ | The Darkening |

In the name of Allah, Most Compassionate, Most Merciful.

بِسۡمِ ٱللَّهِ ٱلرَّحۡمَٰنِ ٱلرَّحِيمِ

1. When the sun will be darkened.[1]

إِذَا ٱلشَّمۡسُ كُوِّرَتۡ ۝

2. And when the stars will lose their light.[2]

وَإِذَا ٱلنُّجُومُ ٱنكَدَرَتۡ ۝

3. And when the mountains will move.[3]

وَإِذَا ٱلۡجِبَالُ سُيِّرَتۡ ۝

4. And when the pregnant she-camel will be left unattended.[4]

وَإِذَا ٱلۡعِشَارُ عُطِّلَتۡ ۝

5. And when the beasts will be gathered.[5]

وَإِذَا ٱلۡوُحُوشُ حُشِرَتۡ ۝

1 – Reference is made to the sunlight illuminating the whole world. However, the sunlight will disappear altogether on the Last Day. The sun stripped of light will appear merely like a piece of cheese.

2 – The stars will fall and lose all their brightness.

3 – The mountains will float into the atmosphere as carded wool.

4 – For the Arabs, the camel is a great treasure. Of the camels, the Arabs value most a ten month pregnant she-camel in that they look forward to the baby camel and plenty of milk. However, on the dreadful Last Day no one will even care about something as precious as the pregnant she-camel. Its master will abandon it altogether.

5 – The reference here is to the beasts which avoid human habitation in mortal fear of man. However, on the Last Day, they will barge into towns and join company with the cattle in utter panic. As calamity strikes, the animals join company with each other, disregarding their traditional enmity. It was observed during

6. And when the oceans will be set boiling.[6]

وَإِذَا ٱلْبِحَارُ سُجِّرَتْ ۝٦

7. And when the souls will be paired.[7]

وَإِذَا ٱلنُّفُوسُ زُوِّجَتْ ۝٧

8. And when the daughter buried alive will be asked,

وَإِذَا ٱلْمَوْءُۥدَةُ سُئِلَتْ ۝٨

9. For what crime was she killed?[8]

بِأَيِّ ذَنۢبٍ قُتِلَتْ ۝٩

10. And when the record will be laid open.

وَإِذَا ٱلصُّحُفُ نُشِرَتْ ۝١٠

a recent flood that the snakes and men took shelter in the same place and the former did not hurt the latter. Likewise, it is common knowledge that in extreme winter beasts look for some refuge in human habitation. Some Qur'ānic scholars hold the expression *Ḥushirat* to be a synonym for Resurrection.

6 – The sea water will evaporate owing to the scorching heat. It will torment unbelievers further in the Hereafter. For the whole place will resemble a blazing hot oven.

7 – Believers and unbelievers will be placed in their respective categories. Likewise, people will be divided into groups on the basis of their faith, conduct and morals. Alternatively, the verse points to the restoration of the soul to the body.

8 – It was once the custom in Arabia for fathers to bury their daughters alive. Some resorted to this out of fear of poverty and their inability to bear the marriage expenses of their daughters. Others could not reconcile themselves to the tie of the son-in-law. The Qur'ān warns that these fathers will be questioned on account of their daughters. They will be asked for what crime their daughters were killed? Parents are not free to do whatever they like to their children. Being parents, they will be subject to a greater punishment for having treated their children so badly.

11. And when the sky will be rent asunder.[9]	وَإِذَا ٱلسَّمَآءُ كُشِطَتْ ۝
12. And when the Hellfire will be set ablaze.[10]	وَإِذَا ٱلْجَحِيمُ سُعِّرَتْ ۝
13. And when the Garden will be brought near.[11]	وَإِذَا ٱلْجَنَّةُ أُزْلِفَتْ ۝
14. Every soul will find out what it brought forth.	عَلِمَتْ نَفْسٌ مَّآ أَحْضَرَتْ ۝
15. So I swear by the receding galaxies.	فَلَآ أُقْسِمُ بِٱلْخُنَّسِ ۝
16. Moving swiftly and hiding themselves.[12]	ٱلْجَوَارِ ٱلْكُنَّسِ ۝
17. And by the night when it spreads.[13]	وَٱلَّيْلِ إِذَا عَسْعَسَ ۝
18. And by the dawn when it breathes.[14]	وَٱلصُّبْحِ إِذَا تَنَفَّسَ ۝

9 – As an animal is skinned after its death, exposing its body completely. By the same token, the gaps in the sky will reveal everything. Smoke will envelope everything, a point which is also made in verse 25 of *Sūrah al-Furqān*.

10 – The Hellfire will rage in its intensity while Paradise will be brought closer to the pious. It will be a delightful spectacle for the latter.

11 – Everyone will come to know about his record of deeds.

12 – Some planets such as Mars, Venus, Saturn and Mercury move in an erratic fashion. At times, they draw very close to the sun and at other times they move very far away.

13 – This might refer to the last phase of the night. The expression used here means both the beginning and the end.

14 – Shāh 'Abdul 'Azīz Muḥaddith Dehlawī observes: "The sun has been likened to fish swimming in water. The spread of its light

19. Verily this is the Word brought by an honourable Messenger

إِنَّهُۥ لَقَوْلُ رَسُولٍ كَرِيمٍ ۝

20. Full of power and holding rank with the Lord of the Throne

ذِى قُوَّةٍ عِندَ ذِى ٱلۡعَرۡشِ مَكِينٍ ۝

21. Everyone is obedient to him. He is trustworthy.[15]

مُّطَاعٍ ثَمَّ أَمِينٍ ۝

prior to the dawn is similar to a fish tail." Or it might refer to the movement of the fish in water. Though it does so with eyes closed, the water is shaken. The same holds true for sunlight before and at dawn. According to some scholars, this stands as a metaphor for the dawn breeze in the spring.

These oaths fit in with the subject matter in the following verse in the sense that the movement and disappearance of the stars corresponds to the phenomenon of Revelation. It is sent down to the Messengers and is then suspended, to be resumed after a long period. Then it stops altogether. The night refers to the darkness of ignorance which preceded the advent of the Prophet Muḥammad ﷺ. Ignorance was so rife in those days that it was hard for people to distinguish between Truth and falsehood. Revelation had lost its meaning and message. The dawn signifies the Prophet's advent. Included in it also is the sending of the Qur'ān in that the light of its guidance illuminated the whole universe. Other Messengers are represented by stars whereas the Prophet Muḥammad ﷺ stands out as the sun radiating Divine Guidance.

According to some other scholars, this parable underscores the appearance and disappearance of angels. The Qur'ān brought an end to the all-round darkness and illuminated the whole universe with its Guidance. This discussion underscores the link in terms of the oath employed in this verse. And Allah knows best.

15 – This is an account of Gabriel's attributes. The Qur'ān has reached mankind through two agencies. The first one is the angel conveying Revelation – Gabriel عليه السلام. The other agency is Prophet Muḥammad ﷺ. In the light of the attributes of both Gabriel عليه السلام and the Prophet ﷺ, one should have no doubt whatever about the Divine

| 22. And this Companion of yours is not mad.[16] | وَمَا صَاحِبُكُم بِمَجْنُونٍ ۝ |
| 23. He did see the angel on the horizon.[17] | وَلَقَدْ رَءَاهُ بِالْأُفُقِ الْمُبِينِ ۝ |

origin and truthfulness of the Qur'ān. Our acceptance of a report depends upon the authenticity and truthfulness of its reporter. If the narrator is honourable, trustworthy, and characterised with features of truthfulness, justice and good memory and is trusted by other reliable people, his report is accepted without reservation. All these features mark Gabriel ﷺ. He is honourable, hence he must be taken as someone pious and purified, as is stated in verse 13 of *Sūrah al-Ḥujurāt*. Furthermore, he is endowed with extraordinary strength. Implicit also is his remarkable capacity for memorising and relating points eloquently. He enjoys an exalted rank with Allah. Of all the angels he enjoys the greatest proximity with Allah. All other angels obey him. Therefore, there should be no doubt whatever about his trustworthiness and reliability. It is followed by an account of the Prophet ﷺ.

16 – Before assuming the office of Messengership, the Prophet ﷺ spent 40 years of his life, day and night, in the company of the Makkans. They, thus, knew first hand his conduct, having witnessed it over such a long period of time. Not once did they note anything odd, immoral or false about his conduct. All along they acknowledged and acclaimed his truthfulness, honesty and sanity. Thus they cannot now dismiss him overnight as a mad person. For he happens to have been their companion for a long period of time, whom they have come to know so well. They betray their own madness in dismissing him as a mad person.

17 – He saw the angel on the eastern horizon in his true form. His vision cannot, therefore, be dismissed as an illusion, in mistaking someone as the angel. This point is also clarified in verse 7 of *Sūrah an-Najm*.

24. He is not miserly in informing about the Unseen[18]	وَمَا هُوَ عَلَى ٱلْغَيْبِ بِضَنِينٍ ٢٤
25. Nor is it the utterance of the accursed Satan.[19]	وَمَا هُوَ بِقَوْلِ شَيْطَٰنٍ رَّجِيمٍ ٢٥
26. Where then are you proceeding?[20]	فَأَيْنَ تَذْهَبُونَ ٢٦
27. This is the reminder for the entire universe.[21]	إِنْ هُوَ إِلَّا ذِكْرٌ لِّلْعَٰلَمِينَ ٢٧

18 – The Prophet ﷺ announces the tidings about the Unseen and about matters related to both the past and the future. He misses no opportunity to instruct people in Divine Attributes, *Sharī'ah* commands, the truth of faith, an account of Paradise and Hell and the tidings of Life-after-Death. He does not demand any wages for providing such information. Nor does he stand in need of offerings. Given this, he cannot be branded as a soothsayer. The latter are known for tampering Truth with falsehood in relating accounts of the Unseen. Furthermore, the latter are so miserly and worldly-minded that they do not instruct anyone in the Unseen, without first asking people to provide them with material things. There is simply no comparison between the Prophet ﷺ and the soothsayers.

19 – Obviously Satan cannot impart the message related to piety and Truth. For it would benefit mankind and lead to his own condemnation.

20 – Since falsehood, madness, flights of imagination and soothsaying are out of the question in the context of the Prophet ﷺ, he embodies only truth. Given this, it is strange that people fall into error while disregarding the Prophet's teachings.

21 – The unbelievers' allegations against the Qur'ān are absolutely false. If they carefully study its subject matter, they would realise that it stands out as the true guidance for all mankind and as a comprehensive code of conduct, ensuring its followers of the best in both worlds.

28. For everyone among you who seeks the straight way.[22]	لِمَن شَآءَ مِنكُمۡ أَن يَسۡتَقِيمَ ۝
29. And you will seek it	وَمَا تَشَآءُونَ
Only when Allah Wills so,	إِلَّآ أَن يَشَآءَ ٱللَّهُ
Lord of all the worlds.[23]	رَبُّ ٱلۡعَٰلَمِينَ ۝

22 – It is the Guidance for those who are inclined to following the straight way. Those following it should abandon all falsehood and hostility. For it benefits only the pious.

23 – The Qur'ān is undoubtedly the source of all Guidance. However, it moves only those whom Allah enables. It transforms some whereas others fail to derive any benefit as a result of their own inability.

* * *

| Al-Infiṭār | سُورَةُ الْاِنْفِطَارِ | The Cleaving |

In the name of Allah, Most Compassionate, Most Merciful.

بِسْمِ اللَّهِ الرَّحْمَنِ الرَّحِيمِ

1. When the sky is rent asunder.

إِذَا السَّمَآءُ انفَطَرَتْ ۝

2. And when the stars disintegrate.

وَإِذَا الْكَوَاكِبُ انتَثَرَتْ ۝

3. And when the oceans overflow.[1]

وَإِذَا الْبِحَارُ فُجِّرَتْ ۝

4. And when the graves are overturned.[2]

وَإِذَا الْقُبُورُ بُعْثِرَتْ ۝

5. Every soul will find out

عَلِمَتْ نَفْسٌ

What it sent forth and what it left behind.[3]

مَّا قَدَّمَتْ وَأَخَّرَتْ ۝

6. O man!

يَٰٓأَيُّهَا الْإِنسَٰنُ

What misleads you against your noble Lord?[4]

مَا غَرَّكَ بِرَبِّكَ الْكَرِيمِ ۝

1 – The sea water will be in turmoil, resulting in the intermingling of bitter and sweet waters.

2 – Whatever lay deep inside the ground will make its appearance. The dead will rise from their graves.

3 – Reference is made to one's deeds, both good and bad, in one's youth or old age. Whether these influenced others or not will also be examined. All these points will become crystal clear on the Day of Judgement.

4 – Allah, being the Most Compassionate Lord, did not deserve to be treated badly by ignorant and arrogant ones. Man should not

7. He Who created you,	اَلَّذِى خَلَقَكَ
Proportioned you and fashioned you.⁵	فَسَوّٰىكَ فَعَدَلَكَ ۝
8. He created you in whatever form He Willed.⁶	فِىٓ أَىِّ صُورَةٍ مَّا شَآءَ رَكَّبَكَ ۝
9. Nay, you reject the Judgement as false.⁷	كَلَّا بَلْ تُكَذِّبُونَ بِالدِّينِ ۝

have repaid His Mercy and favours with disbelief and rebellion. Rather, one should fear Him all the more on noting His numerous bounties. By the same token, one should fear Him, for He is Much Relenting. Of course, Allah is Merciful. However, He exacts justice and is All-Wise. It amounts to nothing but blindness and pride on man's part to disregard His other attributes while focusing only on a single virtue.

5 – Shāh 'Abdul Qādir observes: "Allah has proportioned perfectly the human body. Likewise, He has made man the best in creation. The human body stands out for its proportion and balance, which has been fashioned in a wise manner. Moreover, human nature is a perfect blending of moderation."

6 – Allah has devised distinction in everyone's appearance. Every human being has been blessed with a unique complexion and looks. On the whole, man is superior to all other living beings. Some classical authorities interpret the verse in the sense that had Allah willed, He would have created man in the form of a donkey, dog or even a pig. Thanks to His Mercy man enjoys his present appearance. Since Allah is All Merciful, man should behave reverently towards Him.

7 – There is nothing to deceive man. The unbelievers do not believe in the Day of Judgement. They want to do whatever pleases them. They are averse to any concept of accountability. It does not occur to them that all their deeds are being recorded. For them death is the end of everything.

10. And there are custodians over you.

وَإِنَّ عَلَيْكُمْ لَحَافِظِينَ ﴿١٠﴾

11. Honourable scribes.

كِرَامًا كَاتِبِينَ ﴿١١﴾

12. They know what you do.[8]

يَعْلَمُونَ مَا تَفْعَلُونَ ﴿١٢﴾

13. Verily the virtuous will be in the Gardens.[9]

إِنَّ الْأَبْرَارَ لَفِي نَعِيمٍ ﴿١٣﴾

14. And verily the wicked will be in Hell.

وَإِنَّ الْفُجَّارَ لَفِي جَحِيمٍ ﴿١٤﴾

15. They will be cast in it on the Day of Judgement.

يَصْلَوْنَهَا يَوْمَ الدِّينِ ﴿١٥﴾

16. And they will never be able to depart from it.[10]

وَمَا هُمْ عَنْهَا بِغَائِبِينَ ﴿١٦﴾

17. And do you know what the Day of Judgement is?

وَمَا أَدْرَاكَ مَا يَوْمُ الدِّينِ ﴿١٧﴾

18. Then do you know what the Day of Judgement is?

ثُمَّ مَا أَدْرَاكَ مَا يَوْمُ الدِّينِ ﴿١٨﴾

8 – The reference here is to the angels who do not commit any mistake in performing their duties and in recording man's deeds. Since they have been engaged in compiling the record so faithfully, it will not go to waste. Everyone will be faced with the consequences of his deeds and he will be rewarded or punished for the same. This point is also developed in the following verses.

9 – The dwellers of Paradise will enjoy themselves with Eternal bounties and comforts of all sorts. Had it not been an Eternal Abode, they could not enjoy it at all.

10 – The inmates of Hell cannot escape from it. Once they are hurled into it, there is no way out at all for them. They are destined to Eternal Perdition.

19. The Day when no soul will avail another in any respect.[11]

يَوْمَ لَا تَمْلِكُ نَفْسٌ لِّنَفْسٍ شَيْئًا

And the command that Day will be wholly Allah's.[12]

وَٱلْأَمْرُ يَوْمَئِذٍ لِّلَّهِ ۝

11 – One cannot grasp fully the dread of the Last Day, no matter how seriously one may reflect upon it. In sum, it suffices to say that all blood ties will come to naught on the Day. Everyone will be full of worries on his own account. No one will be able to intercede without the Supreme Lord's leave. Submissiveness, flattery or resolve will not avail man in any degree, except those upon whom Allah showers His Mercy (verse 42 of *Sūrah ad-Dukhān*).

12 – All worldly authorities, as is evident in the relationship between the king and his subjects, parents and their children and master and servant, will come to an end. All authority will belong wholly to the Master of the Universe. He will exercise authority without any partner and in every sense of the term. His dominion will overwhelm everyone.

* * *

In the name of Allah, Most Compassionate, Most Merciful.

بِسْمِ اللَّهِ الرَّحْمَـٰنِ الرَّحِيمِ

1. Woe on those who give short measure.

وَيْلٌ لِّلْمُطَفِّفِينَ ۝

2. Those who when they take

الَّذِينَ إِذَا اكْتَالُوا

   From others, they take in full measure.

عَلَى النَّاسِ يَسْتَوْفُونَ ۝

3. And when they measure

وَإِذَا كَالُوهُمْ

   Or weigh for others, they decrease it.[1]

أَو وَّزَنُوهُمْ يُخْسِرُونَ ۝

4. Do they not think that they will be Resurrected?

أَلَا يَظُنُّ أُولَـٰئِكَ أَنَّهُم مَّبْعُوثُونَ ۝

5. On the Great Day.[2]

لِيَوْمٍ عَظِيمٍ ۝

---

1 – There is no blame, if he insists that his due be granted him. What is condemned is denying this due to anyone. For example, weighing or measuring short is a deplorable act. If one insists on getting an exact measure while one denies the same to others, it is all the more immoral. By comparison, those who forego this right are praiseworthy. The verse makes a pointed reference to weights and measures. It is specifically mentioned that the wicked cheat when they weigh or measure something. The expression *Kail* (measure) used in this context is in line with the customs of Arabia and in Madinah in particular where this was prevalent. It, nonetheless, carries universal import.

2 – Had they been cognisant of Resurrection, when they will have to face the Great Reckoning, they would not have committed any misdeed.

39

6.	The Day mankind will stand	يَوْمَ يَقُومُ ٱلنَّاسُ
	Before the Lord of the entire universe.[3]	لِرَبِّ ٱلْعَٰلَمِينَ ﴿٦﴾
7.	Nay[4] verily the record of the wicked is in the *Sijjīn*.	كَلَّآ إِنَّ كِتَٰبَ ٱلْفُجَّارِ لَفِى سِجِّينٍ ﴿٧﴾
8.	And do you know what *Sijjīn* is?	وَمَآ أَدْرَىٰكَ مَا سِجِّينٌ ﴿٨﴾
9.	It is a written record.[5]	كِتَٰبٌ مَّرْقُومٌ ﴿٩﴾
10.	Woe on that Day for those who reject it as false.	وَيْلٌ يَوْمَئِذٍ لِّلْمُكَذِّبِينَ ﴿١٠﴾
11.	Those who reject the Day of Judgement as false.	ٱلَّذِينَ يُكَذِّبُونَ بِيَوْمِ ٱلدِّينِ ﴿١١﴾

3 – They will look forward to the vision of Allah and to the award of Judgement after the Reckoning.

4 – It should not be supposed that the Day of Judgement will not happen. It is imminent. For this purpose a record of everyone is being maintained.

5 – *Sijjīn* is the record which contains the names of all those to be thrown into Hell. A reference to the angels recording human deeds occurs in *Sūrah al-Infiṭār*. After the death of the wicked, when they are no longer able to commit any deed, their record is preserved, as are their names and it, thus, becomes evident that the deceased is an inmate of Hell. According to some reports, the souls of the unbelievers are also placed aside. Shāh 'Abdul Qādir maintains: "Their names feature in the record and they are destined for Hell after their death. Some classical authorities are of the view that the place reserved for the wicked is below seventh (lowest, most degraded stage of) earth." And Allah knows best.

12. And only those reject it as false who transgress and sin.[6]	وَمَايُكَذِّبُ بِهِۦٓ إِلَّا كُلُّ مُعْتَدٍ أَثِيمٍ ۝
13. And when Our Signs are recited to him,	إِذَا تُتْلَىٰ عَلَيْهِ ءَايَٰتُنَا
He says: "These are the tales of the ancient."[7]	قَالَ أَسَٰطِيرُ ٱلْأَوَّلِينَ ۝
14. Nay, there is a rust upon their hearts	كَلَّا ۖ بَلْ رَانَ عَلَىٰ قُلُوبِهِم
In view of what they did.[8]	مَّا كَانُوا۟ يَكْسِبُونَ ۝

6 – Whoever denies the Day of Judgement, disbelieves in Allah's Lordship, His Omnipotence and His attributes of Justice and Wisdom. Such unbelievers are not shy of committing any misdeed.

7 – Upon listening to the Qur'ān, the unbelievers dismissed it, saying that it recounts only the tales of the ancients. They accused the Prophet ﷺ of having borrowed ancient stories. They blatantly refused to take any heed of these Qur'ānic stories.

8 – No doubt whatever can be entertained regarding Divine Revelation, the hearts of the wicked have been sealed as a result of their frequent indulgences in sin and their indifference to the Truth. As a result, they are unable to appreciate Truth in any degree. It is stated in *Ḥadīth* literature that as one commits a sin, a black spot appears on one's heart. If the person repents, the black spot disappears. Conversely, if he commits other sins, the black spot increases in depth and rootage, ultimately rendering the whole heart black. This makes one unable to distinguish between Truth and falsehood. The same holds true for the Makkan unbelievers in that their hearts have been sealed on account of their consistent sinning. They are, therefore, found to be flagrantly mocking Divine Revelation.

15. Nay, they will be barred on that Day from their Lord.[9]

كَلَّآ إِنَّهُمْ عَن رَّبِّهِمْ يَوْمَئِذٍ لَّمَحْجُوبُونَ ۝

16. Certainly they are to be roasted in Hell.

ثُمَّ إِنَّهُمْ لَصَالُوا الْجَحِيمِ ۝

17. Then it will be said: "This is what you rejected as false."

ثُمَّ يُقَالُ هَٰذَا الَّذِى كُنتُم بِهِۦ تُكَذِّبُونَ ۝

18. Nay,[10] the record of the righteous is in 'Illīyīn.

كَلَّآ إِنَّ كِتَٰبَ الْأَبْرَارِ لَفِى عِلِّيِّينَ ۝

19. And do you know what 'Illīyīn is?

وَمَآ أَدْرَىٰكَ مَا عِلِّيُّونَ ۝

20. It is a written record.[11]

كِتَٰبٌ مَّرْقُومٌ ۝

21. Those near Him witness it.[12]

يَشْهَدُهُ الْمُقَرَّبُونَ ۝

22. Verily the righteous will be in utmost comfort.

إِنَّ الْأَبْرَارَ لَفِى نَعِيمٍ ۝

9 – The unbelievers should not disregard the consequences of their rejection and unbelief. Soon there will be a time when the Believers will be blessed with the vision of Allah the Almighty whereas the wicked unbelievers will be deprived of this privilege.

10 – The wicked and the Believers will not and cannot be treated alike.

11 – The record of the dwellers of Paradise is also being maintained. This fact is indicated on their individual records. Their souls are transported there. Moreover, these blessed souls maintain a direct link with their graves. It is said that this place is located above the seventh heaven and is inhabited by the souls of those who have gained proximity with Allah. And Allah knows best.

12 – The near angels, or such servants of Allah who are close to Him, study this record of Believers and rejoice in it.

23. They will be watching
while reclining on couches.[13]

عَلَى ٱلْأَرَآئِكِ يَنظُرُونَ ﴿٢٣﴾

24. You will recognise in their faces

تَعْرِفُ فِى وُجُوهِهِمْ

The brightness
because of delight.[14]

نَضْرَةَ ٱلنَّعِيمِ ﴿٢٤﴾

25. They will be offered drink,
pure and sealed.[15]

يُسْقَوْنَ مِن رَّحِيقٍ مَّخْتُومٍ ﴿٢٥﴾

26. It is sealed with musk[16]

خِتَـٰمُهُۥ مِسْكٌ

And for this let those aspire
who have aspiration.[17]

وَفِى ذَٰلِكَ فَلْيَتَنَافَسِ ٱلْمُتَنَافِسُونَ ﴿٢٦﴾

27. And it is mixed
with the water of *Tasnīm*.

وَمِزَاجُهُۥ مِن تَسْنِيمٍ ﴿٢٧﴾

13 – Seated on couches, they will enjoy their stay in Paradise. Furthermore, their eyes will be cooled with the vision of the Almighty.

14 – As a result of the joys of Paradise available to the dwellers therein, their faces will reflect a unique freshness. Upon looking at them it will be readily observable to everyone that they are enjoying themselves.

15 – Shāh ʿAbdul Qādir writes: "The rivers of wine will flow in every palace in Paradise. This verse, however, refers to a rare, sealed wine."

16 – Just as clay or some other material is used for sealing, musk will be used for the same purpose in Paradise. As a result, as one takes a cup of drink, fragrance will overcome one. This will be an ever-lasting fragrance.

17 – As for the wine in this world, it is so pernicious that the pious should not even look at it, only the pure wine of Paradise is suitable for them. The Believers should vie with one other to acquire this drink.

28. It is a spring
of which those drink

Who are brought near Him.[18]

عَيْنًا يَشْرَبُ بِهَا ٱلْمُقَرَّبُونَ ﴿٢٨﴾

29. Verily the sinners used to

Laugh at those who
believed the Believers.[19]

إِنَّ ٱلَّذِينَ أَجْرَمُوا۟ كَانُوا۟ مِنَ ٱلَّذِينَ ءَامَنُوا۟ يَضْحَكُونَ ﴿٢٩﴾

30. And when they passed by them,
they winked at them.[20]

وَإِذَا مَرُّوا۟ بِهِمْ يَتَغَامَزُونَ ﴿٣٠﴾

31. And when they returned
to their homes,

They turned away
and told lies.[21]

وَإِذَا ٱنقَلَبُوٓا۟ إِلَىٰٓ أَهْلِهِمُ ٱنقَلَبُوا۟ فَكِهِينَ ﴿٣١﴾

32. And when they saw them,

They said:
"Verily they are in error."[22]

وَإِذَا رَأَوْهُمْ قَالُوٓا۟ إِنَّ هَٰٓؤُلَآءِ لَضَآلُّونَ ﴿٣٢﴾

18 – The pious will be offered this drink. It will be tempered with fragrances.

19 – The unbelievers mocked the Believers for their looking forward to the joys of Paradise. It seemed strange to them that the latter forego all worldly pleasures for the sake of joys promised to them in Paradise.

20 – The unbelievers think that the Believers are fools in sacrificing worldly joys and in looking forward to the bounties of Paradise.

21 – The unbelievers used to mock the Muslims and were too proud of their worldly possessions and luxury. They thought that if they had not been in the right, they would not have been blessed with such prosperity.

22 – They deride the Believers for their self-restraint and for their preference for the joys of Paradise to worldly pleasures. They regard

33. And they were not sent
as custodians over them.[23]

وَمَآ أُرْسِلُوا۟ عَلَيْهِمْ حَٰفِظِينَ ۝

34. That Day the Believers

فَٱلْيَوْمَ ٱلَّذِينَ ءَامَنُوا۟

Will mock the unbelievers.[24]

مِنَ ٱلْكُفَّارِ يَضْحَكُونَ ۝

35. They will watch reclining
on their couches.[25]

عَلَى ٱلْأَرَآئِكِ يَنظُرُونَ ۝

36. Now, the unbelievers
receive the recompense

هَلْ ثُوِّبَ ٱلْكُفَّارُ

For what they used to do.[26]

مَا كَانُوا۟ يَفْعَلُونَ ۝

abandoning the ancestral faith and undergoing persecution in the cause of the new faith as error.

23 – Allah tells the unbelievers that they are not the Believers' custodians. It is not their responsibility to watch or criticise the latter's conduct. It is indeed strange in that they do not care about mending their own ways yet they abuse their time and energy in condemning the Believers.

24 – On the Day of Judgement, it will be the turn of the Believers to laugh at the unbelievers. They will make fun of the latter's myopic vision and foolishness in having preferred this world to the Next Life. The unbelievers will suffer Eternal Perdition.

25 – The Believers will witness their own prosperity and the unbelievers' sufferings on the Day of Judgement.

26 – Those who mock the Believers will be in utter misery on the Day of Judgement. The former will laugh at the latter.

* * *

Al-Inshiqāq — سورة الانشقاق — The Splitting Asunder

In the name of Allah, Most Compassionate, Most Merciful.

1. When the sky is rent asunder.[1]

إِذَا السَّمَآءُ انشَقَّتْ ۝١

2. And listens to its Lord and it befits it.

وَأَذِنَتْ لِرَبِّهَا وَحُقَّتْ ۝٢

3. And when the earth is flattened out.[2]

وَإِذَا الْأَرْضُ مُدَّتْ ۝٣

4. And it brings out whatever and turns empty.[3]

وَأَلْقَتْ مَا فِيهَا وَتَخَلَّتْ ۝٤

5. When it listens to its Lord and it befits it.[4]

وَأَذِنَتْ لِرَبِّهَا وَحُقَّتْ ۝٥

1 – When Allah decides that it is time to bring an end to the present order, all objects of the universe will readily follow His command. Since Allah is All-Powerful and all objects are the created and helpless ones, it is mandatory upon them to surrender themselves wholly to the Lord. They cannot dare disobey Him in the least.

2 – On the Last Day, the earth will be flattened, all the mountains and structures levelled. On this level ground everyone will stand. There will be no barrier to separate one from another.

3 – The earth will throw up all its treasures on the Last Day. It will render a perfectly true account of all human deeds.

4 – Since the heavens and earth are completely governed by Allah, it does not befit man to disobey His commands.

6. O man! You have to undergo some hardship	يَٰٓأَيُّهَا ٱلْإِنسَٰنُ إِنَّكَ كَادِحٌ
In reaching your Lord. You have to meet Him.[5]	إِلَىٰ رَبِّكَ كَدْحًا فَمُلَٰقِيهِ ۝
7. So who is given his record in his right hand.	فَأَمَّا مَنْ أُوتِىَ كِتَٰبَهُۥ بِيَمِينِهِۦ ۝
8. He will be subject to a light reckoning.[6]	فَسَوْفَ يُحَاسَبُ حِسَابًا يَسِيرًا ۝
9. And he will return to his people, rejoicing.[7]	وَيَنقَلِبُ إِلَىٰٓ أَهْلِهِۦ مَسْرُورًا ۝
10. And who is given his record from behind his back.[8]	وَأَمَّا مَنْ أُوتِىَ كِتَٰبَهُۥ وَرَآءَ ظَهْرِهِۦ ۝
11. He will ask for death.[9]	فَسَوْفَ يَدْعُواْ ثُبُورًا ۝

5 – Everyone strives in his own way before his death. There are some who undergo serious hardships in obeying their Lord. Then there are those who spend all their energy on doing evil. After completing life, be it good or evil, one will ultimately return to the Lord and face the consequences of one's deeds.

6 – Man may not be taken to task for each and every minor lapse. His whole record will be presented and the Believers will be spared, without being subjected to any ordeal.

7 – The Believers will not fear nor grieve. They will join company with other Believers and their kith and kin in utter delight, peace and security.

8 – The wicked will be handed their record of deeds from behind their backs. The angels will not even like to look at them. It will indicate their revulsion for the wicked. Given that it is also likely that the wicked will be in fetters, they will necessarily be given their record in the above manner.

9 – The unbelievers will ask for death out of their fear of Divine punishment.

12. And he will be hurled into the blazing fire.	وَيَصْلَىٰ سَعِيرًا ۝
13. Verily he had lived among his people, rejoicing.[10]	إِنَّهُۥ كَانَ فِىٓ أَهْلِهِۦ مَسْرُورًا ۝
14. He thought that he will not have to return.[11]	إِنَّهُۥ ظَنَّ أَن لَّن يَحُورَ ۝
15. Nay, his Lord did watch him.[12]	بَلَىٰٓ إِنَّ رَبَّهُۥ كَانَ بِهِۦ بَصِيرًا ۝
16. So I swear by the twilight.	فَلَآ أُقْسِمُ بِٱلشَّفَقِ ۝
17. And by the night when things are gathered into it.[13]	وَٱلَّيْلِ وَمَا وَسَقَ ۝

10 – Since the unbelievers were negligent of the Hereafter, they will have to suffer much on the Day of Judgement. By contrast, those who were all along concerned about their ultimate end will have total peace and security. The unbelievers may enjoy themselves in this life. However, the Believers will be blessed with Eternal happiness in the Hereafter.

11 – It never occurred to the unbelievers that one day they will have to render their account to their Lord and be answerable for each and every deed. Accordingly, they indulge in sin without any scruple.

12 – Man will be asked whether he reflected on the various phases of his life, from birth to death, the origin of his soul, the constituents of his body, his articles of Faith and his record of deeds. He will be questioned thoroughly about his intentions, his utterances and his actions. Man should contemplate upon the final abode and on the decomposition of his dead body.

Since Allah is fully familiar with each and every deed of man, it is unthinkable that He will let man go scot-free. It is imperative that He punishes or rewards man for his deeds.

13 – Reference is made here to men and animals who go out every morning, seeking their sustenance; at dusk they return home.

18. And by the moon when it is at the full.[14]	وَٱلْقَمَرِ إِذَا ٱتَّسَقَ ۝
19. That you have to ascend, stage by stage.[15]	لَتَرْكَبُنَّ طَبَقًا عَن طَبَقٍ ۝
20. What has happened to them that they do not believe.[16]	فَمَا لَهُمْ لَا يُؤْمِنُونَ ۝
21. And when the Qur'ān is recited to them,	وَإِذَا قُرِئَ عَلَيْهِمُ ٱلْقُرْءَانُ
They do not prostrate.[17]	لَا يَسْجُدُونَ ۩ ۝
22. Nay, they are the ones who reject it as false.	بَلِ ٱلَّذِينَ كَفَرُوا يُكَذِّبُونَ ۝

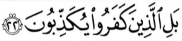

14 – That is the full moon which is remarkable for its splendour.

15 – The reference is to the various phases of man's life, which culminates in death. It is followed by the phases of *Barzakh*, and the Day of Judgement. On the Day of Reckoning itself man will undergo numerous phases. By the same analogy, a special light illuminates the sky from late evening till dawn, pointing to the remnants of the sunlight. As twilight disappears altogether, darkness envelops everything. Then the moon rises and its light gradually increases. On the fourteenth of every month the moon appears in its utmost glory and overcomes the darkness of the night completely. Thus, the numerous stages of human life correspond with the various stages of night itself. And Allah knows best.

16 – We have to return to Allah after death. Everyone has to undertake this arduous journey. Therefore, everyone should make preparations for the journey.

17 – If they could not perceive the Truth on their own, they should have drawn upon the Guidance provided by the Qur'ān. However, on listening to the Qur'ān, the unbelievers did not act with any humility. Even when the Muslims prostrate on listening to the Qur'ānic verses, they are unmoved.

23. And Allah knows well what is inside them.[18]

وَٱللَّهُ أَعْلَمُ بِمَا يُوعُونَ ۝

24. So announce to them the "Glad" Tidings of the terrible punishment.[19]

فَبَشِّرْهُم بِعَذَابٍ أَلِيمٍ ۝

25. Except those who believe and do good.

إِلَّا ٱلَّذِينَ ءَامَنُوا۟ وَعَمِلُوا۟ ٱلصَّٰلِحَٰتِ

There is immeasurable reward for them.[20]

لَهُمْ أَجْرٌ غَيْرُ مَمْنُونٍ ۝

18 – Not only are they disregardful of these Divine verses and fail to display humility towards them, they exceed all the limits in rejecting the Qur'ān as false. Allah knows well their unbelief, rejection, hostility and aversion to Truth.

19 – The Prophet ﷺ is directed to announce the 'Glad Tidings' to the unbelievers that they will certainly be recompensed for their deeds.

20 – Their reward will be unending.

* * *

Al-Burūj	The Big Stars

In the name of Allah, Most Compassionate, Most Merciful.	
1. By the sky in which there are constellations.[1]	وَٱلسَّمَآءِ ذَاتِ ٱلْبُرُوجِ ١
2. And by the Promised Day.[2]	وَٱلْيَوْمِ ٱلْمَوْعُودِ ٢
3. And by the witness and what is witnessed.[3]	وَشَاهِدٍ وَمَشْهُودٍ ٣
4. The People of the Ditch have been destroyed.	قُتِلَ أَصْحَٰبُ ٱلْأُخْدُودِ ٤

1 – Reference is made to either the twelve constellations through which the sun passes in a year or it stands for the celestial castles guarded by the angels. Alternatively, it might refer to the large stars visible in the sky. And Allah knows best.

2 – That is the Day of Judgement.

3 – Friday is the Day of Testimony. All Believers assemble on the Day of *Ḥajj* at 'Arafāt. Accordingly, the Qur'ānic expressions *Shāhid* and *Mashhūd* are taken to mean Friday and the Day at 'Arafāt respectively. These expressions have been variously interpreted. However, the above interpretation is more plausible. And Allah knows best.

We have already discussed in the opening part of *Sūrah al-Qiyāmah* the issue of Qur'ānic oaths. This should now be studied afresh. These oaths bring out the Lordship, Omnipotence and other attributes of Allah. Those who oppose Him obviously stand accursed and deserving of a terrible punishment.

5. The Fire, full of intense fuel.[4]	ٱلنَّارِ ذَاتِ ٱلۡوَقُودِ ٥
6. When they sat by it.	إِذۡ هُمۡ عَلَيۡهَا قُعُودٌ ٦

4 – The cursed are those who dug trenches and filled them with fire and fuel. The Qur'ānic scholars have presented many views about the identity of *Aṣḥāb al-Ukhdūd* (the People of Ukhdūd). On the basis of their story which is featured in *Ṣaḥīḥ Muslim, Jāmeʿ Tirmidhī*, and *Musnad Aḥmad*, the following salient details emerge.

A long time ago there was an unbelieving king who had a magician as his courtier. As the latter was about to die, he requested the former to provide him with an intelligent youth as his apprentice. This so as to preserve his special knowledge. A suitable youth was identified. He used to visit the magician every day to learn his art and craft. On route, there lived a devout Christian monk. He observed the faith of the day. The same youth also started to visit the monk every day. He embraced faith at the monk's hands. By his blessings the youth was elevated to a high spiritual rank. One day the youth found his way obstructed by a beast, who had caused terror in the whole region. The youth picked up a stone and invoked Allah thus: "O God! If the monk's faith is genuine, let this beast be killed by me." While saying this he threw the stone at the beast, and this killed it. Reports spread far and wide that the youth possessed special knowledge. A blind person approached him, requesting him to restore his eyesight. The youth, however, clarified that he did not possess any such authority. For only the One True God could accomplish this. Was the blind person to embrace Faith in Him, make a supplication, then God might restore his eyesight. This is exactly what happened. Gradually, these reports reached the king. Enraged, he summoned the youth, the monk and the cured blind person. After having a summary trial, the king executed both the monk and the blind person. He commanded that the youth be thrown down from a hilltop. However, those who had carried the youth to the mountain were themselves killed whereas the youth returned unharmed.

7.	And what they did	وَهُمْ عَلَىٰ مَا يَفْعَلُونَ
	Against the Believers were witnessed by themselves.[5]	بِالْمُؤْمِنِينَ شُهُودٌ ۞
8.	And they persecuted them for only that they believed	وَمَا نَقَمُوا مِنْهُمْ إِلَّا أَن يُؤْمِنُوا
	In Allah, Almighty, Most Praiseworthy.	بِاللَّهِ الْعَزِيزِ الْحَمِيدِ ۞

Then the king directed that the boy be drowned in the sea. Exactly what had happened earlier again followed. For the youth was saved whereas those deputised to kill him were themselves killed. Eventually, the youth said that he could himself tell the king how he could be put to death. The king should arrange for a grand public gathering and tie him to a pillar and shoot him with an arrow while saying: "In the name of Allah, the Lord of the youth."

The king followed his directions and the youth sacrificed his life in the cause of Allah. On witnessing this amazing spectacle all those present at the site of his execution exclaimed: "All of us embrace faith in the Lord of the youth." What the king wanted to avoid though did happen. For people accepted Faith in large numbers, notwithstanding his displeasure. Before the youth's execution only a few people had embraced the Faith. However, his sacrifice led to the acceptance of Faith on a large scale. Enraged, the king directed that large trenches be dug and filled with fire and fuel. Then he proclaimed that whoever embraces Faith should be hurled into these trenches. Many were thrown into the trenches, yet they did not renounce their Faith. There appeared a believing woman with a suckling baby in her arms. She hesitated momentarily on account of her baby. However, Allah directed the baby to tell the mother: "O my mother! Be patient. You are in the right."

5 – The king and his courtiers callously watched the burning of the Believers in the trenches. They were not moved at all by this ghastly scene.

9. Whose is the dominion of the heavens and the earth	ٱلَّذِى لَهُۥ مُلْكُ ٱلسَّمَٰوَٰتِ وَٱلْأَرْضِ
And Allah is a witness over everything.[6]	وَٱللَّهُ عَلَىٰ كُلِّ شَىْءٍ شَهِيدٌ ٩
10. Those who persecuted Believing men and women	إِنَّ ٱلَّذِينَ فَتَنُوا۟ ٱلْمُؤْمِنِينَ وَٱلْمُؤْمِنَٰتِ
And did not repent, there is the punishment of Hell for them.	ثُمَّ لَمْ يَتُوبُوا۟ فَلَهُمْ عَذَابُ جَهَنَّمَ
And there is a punishment of the blazing Fire for them.[7]	وَلَهُمْ عَذَابُ ٱلْحَرِيقِ ١٠
11. Verily those who believe	إِنَّ ٱلَّذِينَ ءَامَنُوا۟
And do good,	وَعَمِلُوا۟ ٱلصَّٰلِحَٰتِ

6 – The only crime of these Believers was that they had embraced Faith in Allah Who deserves all worship and that they had moved away from the darkness of unbelief into the Light of Faith. Allah's Omnipotence is beyond question. Since He knows each and everything, He could not silently watch the execution of His true Believers on account of their Faith. Allah is bound to punish such oppressors and enemies of Truth. Shāh 'Abdul Qādir Dehlawī elaborates: "As Divine punishment overtook them, the same fire spread into their town, reducing the royal palaces to ashes." This point is not, however, supported by authentic reports. All praise be to Allah Who knows best.

7 – This Truth is not specific to the People of the Trenches. All those who persecute Believers on account of their Faith, as was the case with the Makkan unbelievers, and who do not mend their ways, are doomed for Hellfire. They will be subject to numerous hardships and punishment by fire. The enemies of Truth will ultimately be in a miserable condition.

There are Gardens for them beneath which rivers flow.	لَهُمْ جَنَّٰتٌ تَجْرِى مِن تَحْتِهَا ٱلْأَنْهَٰرُ
This is the supreme achievement.[8]	ذَٰلِكَ ٱلْفَوْزُ ٱلْكَبِيرُ ۝
12. Verily the grip of your Lord is severe.[9]	إِنَّ بَطْشَ رَبِّكَ لَشَدِيدٌ ۝
13. Verily He it is Who originates and resurrects.[10]	إِنَّهُۥ هُوَ يُبْدِئُ وَيُعِيدُ ۝
14. And He is Most Forgiving, Most Affectionate.[11]	وَهُوَ ٱلْغَفُورُ ٱلْوَدُودُ ۝
15. Lord of the Throne, Most Glorious.	ذُو ٱلْعَرْشِ ٱلْمَجِيدُ ۝
16. He accomplishes what He intends.[12]	فَعَّالٌ لِّمَا يُرِيدُ ۝

8 – The Believers are directed not to be discouraged by their hardship and suffering. They are destined for ultimate success. As compared to their abiding reward, their present plight is very light.

9 – Allah inflicts a severe punishment upon wrongdoers and the wicked.

10 – Reference is made to their punishment in this life and in the Hereafter (*Mūḍiḥ al-Qur'ān*). Alternatively, it might mean that Allah creates man in the first place and He resurrects him after his death. Therefore, the unbelievers should not suffer from the delusion that they will not be brought to book once they die and their bodies decompose.

11 – Notwithstanding His punishment and wrath, Allah's Mercy and Grace is boundless. He overlooks numerous lapses of His faithful servants and bestows upon them a variety of favours and bounties.

12 – It does not take any time for Allah to accomplish whatever He intends out of His Perfect Knowledge and Wisdom. No one can question His actions. Nonetheless, a servant should not be proud of the Divine bounties showered upon him. Nor should he become

17. Did the tidings of those armies not reach you?	هَلۡ أَتَىٰكَ حَدِيثُ ٱلۡجُنُودِ ۝
18. Of Pharaoh and Thamūd.[13]	فِرۡعَوۡنَ وَثَمُودَ ۝
19. Nay, only the unbelievers deny it.[14]	بَلِ ٱلَّذِينَ كَفَرُواْ فِى تَكۡذِيبٍ ۝
20. And Allah has embraced them on all sides.[15]	وَٱللَّهُ مِن وَرَآئِهِم مُّحِيطُۢ ۝
21. Nay, it is the Qur'ān, most praiseworthy.[16]	بَلۡ هُوَ قُرۡءَانٌ مَّجِيدٌ ۝
22. Recorded in the Guarded Tablet.[17]	فِى لَوۡحٍ مَّحۡفُوظِۭ ۝

fearless about His punishment. Believers keep in mind both the Glory and Mercy of Allah. They are full of hope and fear with regard to Allah. A perfect balance between hope and fear should fill the hearts of Believers.

13 – For long they were favoured with Divine bounties. A variety of Divine favours were showered upon them. However, they were severely punished on account of their unbelief and rebellion.

14 – The unbelievers do not take any lesson from these stories. They are not at all afraid of Divine punishment. Rather, they abuse their talent and energy in rejecting these Qur'ānic stories as false.

15 – Their rejection of Truth is pointless. In so doing, they incur only Divine punishment. They cannot escape Allah's grip or His punishment.

16 – Likewise, their rejection of the Qur'ān is pointless. The Qur'ān is too elevated to be dismissed. Its denial by a handful of unbelievers does not take away its abiding glory.

17 – The Guarded Tablet is unalterable. It was from there that Divine Revelation was communicated to the Prophet ﷺ in a perfectly safe fashion. Almost the same point is made in verse 27 of *Sūrah al-Jinn*. Allah has devised such a complete security system for the transmission of Qur'ānic Revelation that no power on earth can tamper with it.

Aṭ-Ṭāriq	سُوْرَةُ الطَّارِقِ	The Night Visitant

In the name of Allah, Most Compassionate, Most Merciful.

بِسْمِ اللهِ الرَّحْمٰنِ الرَّحِيْمِ

1. By the sky and the night visitant.

وَالسَّمَاءِ وَالطَّارِقِ ۝

2. And do you know what the night visitant is?

وَمَا أَدْرٰىكَ مَا الطَّارِقُ ۝

3. It is a shining star.

اَلنَّجْمُ الثَّاقِبُ ۝

4. For every living being there is a custodian.[1]

إِنْ كُلُّ نَفْسٍ لَّمَّا عَلَيْهَا حَافِظٌ ۝

5. So see, of what is man created?

فَلْيَنْظُرِ الْإِنْسَانُ مِمَّ خُلِقَ ۝

6. Created of a flowing fluid.[2]

خُلِقَ مِنْ مَّاءٍ دَافِقٍ ۝

1 – The angels accompany man in that they defend him against calamity and record his deeds (Mūḍiḥ al-Qur'ān). Implicit in this oath is the point that Allah Who has arranged for the security of the stars in the sky, does not find it at all hard to record man's deeds. Furthermore, the stars enjoy a safe, secure existence. However, they make their appearance only at night. By the same token, man's record of deeds is fully preserved, to be declared publicly on a certain day, the Day of Reckoning. Given this, man should feel duly concerned about the Hereafter. He should reflect upon his birth and his return to the Hereafter.

2 – The reference here is to semen which is ejaculated.

7.	Which comes out of the loins and breast-bones.[3]	يَخْرُجُ مِنۢ بَيْنِ ٱلصُّلْبِ وَٱلتَّرَآئِبِ ٧
8.	Verily He is capable of Resurrection.[4]	إِنَّهُۥ عَلَىٰ رَجْعِهِۦ لَقَادِرٌ ٨
9.	The Day when the secrets will be out.[5]	يَوْمَ تُبْلَى ٱلسَّرَآئِرُ ٩
10.	For man there will not be any help or supporter.[6]	فَمَا لَهُۥ مِن قُوَّةٍ وَلَا نَاصِرٍ ١٠
11.	By the sky that revolves.[7]	وَٱلسَّمَآءِ ذَاتِ ٱلرَّجْعِ ١١
12.	And the earth bursting with vegetation.	وَٱلْأَرْضِ ذَاتِ ٱلصَّدْعِ ١٢
13.	Verily this is the clear word.	إِنَّهُۥ لَقَوْلٌ فَصْلٌ ١٣

3 – It is said that semen originates from the loin in the case of a male and from the chest in the case of a female. Some scholars hold that these body parts are mentioned metaphorically. For semen is produced by the whole body and is released during sexual intercourse. Special mention of these bodily parts is made in view of the strong association of the heart, the mind and the belly with sexual activity. And Allah knows best.

4 – Allah will resurrect mankind (Mūḍiḥ al-Qur'ān). Creating man from a drop of semen is much more wonderful than resurrecting man. Since Allah has already created something in amazing fashion, it is ridiculous to hold that He cannot do something which is not so difficult.

5 – Everyone will stand exposed there. What one held even in the depths of one's heart or which one committed publicly will be declared. No crime will remain concealed.

6 – The wicked will not be able to defend themselves. Nor will they have any helper to support them.

7 – Or which brings rain.

14. And it is not something for amusement.[8]	وَمَا هُوَ بِٱلْهَزْلِ ۝
15. However, they are given to plots.	إِنَّهُمْ يَكِيدُونَ كَيْدًا ۝
16. And I engaged in My strategy.	وَأَكِيدُ كَيْدًا ۝
17. So grant respite to the unbelievers.	فَمَهِّلِ ٱلْكَٰفِرِينَ
Grant them a little respite.[9]	أَمْهِلْهُمْ رُوَيْدًا ۝

8 – The Qur'ānic statements about the Hereafter are not to be taken lightly. The Qur'ān illustrates the sharp distinction between Truth and falsehood. Undoubtedly, it is Truth and it announces Tidings which are bound to happen.

Note: The co-relation between the oath and the subject matter is that the Qur'ān descends from the heavens, as is the case with rainfall. Whoever has receptivity benefits immensely from both the Qur'ān and rain water. For the latter infuses a new life into dry, barren land. By the same analogy, there will be a Divine rainfall on the Day of Judgement, restoring the dead to life in the manner rain water brings back the dead land to life and fills it with life and activity.

9 – It is the strategy of the unbelievers to raise and circulate doubts about the Truth lest it might spread. However, Divine strategy is also at work, and it is not perceived by unbelievers. As a result, their conspiracy will come to naught and the tables will be turned upon them. It is for them to think how their conspiracy can work against Allah, the Lord of everything. These unbelievers are bound to fail and suffer. The Prophet ﷺ should not, therefore, ask that they be punished at an early date. Nor should he be provoked by their misdeeds into cursing them. Rather, the unbelievers should be granted a respite in order for them to reach a logical conclusion.

| Al-A'lā | سُوْرَةُ الْأَعْلَى | The Most High |

In the name of Allah, Most Compassionate, Most Merciful.

1. Celebrate the Name of your Lord, Most High.[1]

سَبِّحِ اسْمَ رَبِّكَ الْأَعْلَى ۝

2. He Who has created and proportioned.[2]

الَّذِيْ خَلَقَ فَسَوَّى ۝

3. And He Who has fashioned and guided.[3]

وَالَّذِيْ قَدَّرَ فَهَدَى ۝

4. And He Who has brought forth pasturage.

وَالَّذِيْٓ اَخْرَجَ الْمَرْعَى ۝

5. Then He reduced it to dusky stubble.[4]

فَجَعَلَهُ غُثَآءً اَحْوَى ۝

1 – It is stated that when this verse was revealed, the Prophet ﷺ directed Muslims to recite the same while they prostrated. Accordingly, it is recited in this manner while one prays.

2 – All objects created by Allah are characterised by balance and excellence. All objects fulfill the purpose of their creation. Allah has perfected everything and invested it with such moderation that it delivers the goods in the desired manner.

3 – Shāh 'Abdul Qādir says: "Allah has decreed everything and brought everything into being." In other words, Allah provides guidance to everyone. Shāh 'Abdul 'Azīz maintains: "Allah has preordained a measure for everyone's perfection and guided him on how to attain the same."

4 – First, beautiful lush green grass comes out of the soil. This is gradually reduced into stubble and serves as fodder for cattle.

6. Verily We will enable you to recite and you will not forget it.	سَنُقْرِئُكَ فَلَا تَنسَىٰ ٦
7. Except what Allah Wills.[5]	إِلَّا مَا شَآءَ ٱللَّهُ
Verily He knows the manifest and what is hidden.[6]	إِنَّهُۥ يَعْلَمُ ٱلْجَهْرَ وَمَا يَخْفَىٰ ٧
8. And We will facilitate for you the easy way.[7]	وَنُيَسِّرُكَ لِلْيُسْرَىٰ ٨
9. So admonish if the admonition benefits.[8]	فَذَكِّرْ إِن نَّفَعَتِ ٱلذِّكْرَىٰ ٩

5 – Allah has created and guided everything to its perfection. In like manner, Allah will instruct the Prophet ﷺ gradually in the Qur'ān and infuse it so well into his heart that he will not forget any part of it, except such verses which are meant to be forgotten and so abrogated.

6 – Allah knows both the open and secret acts of everything and will recompense everyone accordingly. There should not be any doubt with regard to the abrogation of verses which have been revealed. Allah Alone knows in His Wisdom its rationale. Since His Knowledge embraces everything, He knows best what is to be retained and what is to be abrogated. Likewise, He knows well what is to be preserved only up to a certain point of time and which is then to be withdrawn after having served its assigned role.

7 – Allah will facilitate man's remembrance of Revelation. Moreover, he will find it easy to gain Allah's gnosis, modes of worship and affairs of the world. All obstacles will be removed.

8 – Allah has granted the Prophet ﷺ much favour. He should help others in gaining perfection. Verse 9 of this *Sūrah* specifies that preaching is to be done when the addressees are likely to respond positively to it. Not everyone can carry out the mission of preaching in the manner of the Prophet ﷺ. Some Qur'ānic scholars interpret the verse in the sense that the advice should be given repeatedly, if

10. He who fears will take admonition.[9]	سَيَذَّكَّرُ مَن يَخْشَىٰ ﴿١٠﴾
11. However, the unfortunate one will turn away from it.	وَيَتَجَنَّبُهَا ٱلْأَشْقَى ﴿١١﴾
12. He will be admitted to the Great Fire.[10]	ٱلَّذِى يَصْلَى ٱلنَّارَ ٱلْكُبْرَىٰ ﴿١٢﴾
13. There he will neither die nor live in it.[11]	ثُمَّ لَا يَمُوتُ فِيهَا وَلَا يَحْيَىٰ ﴿١٣﴾
14. Verily who has purified himself prospers.[12]	قَدْ أَفْلَحَ مَن تَزَكَّىٰ ﴿١٤﴾
15. And mentions the name of his Lord and prays.[13]	وَذَكَرَ ٱسْمَ رَبِّهِ فَصَلَّىٰ ﴿١٥﴾

it does not work the first time. That the Truth should be preached repeatedly implies that it will eventually benefit the addressees. Almost the same point is made in verse 55 of *Sūrah adh-Dhāriyāt*. Since the preaching of Truth is essential for man, it has to be carried out consistently and regularly.

9 – Only such are admonished and take heed who fear Allah and who are concerned about their ultimate end.

10 – Those destined for Hellfire fail to grasp the Truth. Since they do not fear Allah or their punishment in the Hereafter, they behave indifferently towards the admonition and do not pay any attention to Truth.

11 – The unbelievers will not die, for this would put an end to their plight. Nor will they enjoy any comfort. Their life will be so miserable that they will wish for death. May Allah protect us against this.

12 – Reference is made to the one who is free from both outward and inward impurity. His heart is adorned by sound beliefs, excellent morals and good deeds.

13 – Believers purify themselves and glorify Allah. They offer Prayers. According to some classical authorities, verses 14 and 15 of

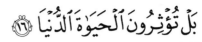
16. Nay, you prefer the life of this world.	بَل تُؤثِرُونَ الحَيَوٰةَ الدُّنيَا ﴿١٦﴾
17. While the Hereafter is better and lasting.[14]	وَالأَخِرَةُ خَيرٌ وَأَبقَىٰ ﴿١٧﴾
18. This is recorded in the earlier scrolls.	إِنَّ هَٰذَا لَفِى الصُّحُفِ الأُولَىٰ ﴿١٨﴾
19. In the scrolls of Abraham and Moses.[15]	صُحُفِ إِبرَٰهِيمَ وَمُوسَىٰ ﴿١٩﴾

this *Sūrah* contain allusion to *Zakāh*, *Ṣadaqah al-Fiṭr* and the extra invocations in the '*Īd* Prayers.

14 – The unbelievers cannot enjoy any good in that they are indifferent to the Hereafter. Rather, they are guilty of preferring worldly life to the Hereafter. They are more concerned about their worldly joys. In so doing they fail to realise that this worldly life is inferior and ephemeral. By comparison, the Next Life is abiding and better. It is indeed strange that they should prefer something inferior to that which is decidedly superior in every respect.

15 – The import of this verse also features in the earlier Scriptures. This abiding Truth has never been abrogated or altered. The point is, therefore, made very forcefully. According to some inauthentic reports, ten scrolls were sent down to the Prophet Abraham ﷺ and another ten to the Prophet Moses ﷺ in addition to the Torah. It is difficult, however, to ascertain the truth of this report.

* * *

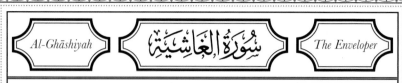

Al-Ghāshiyah سُورَةُ الغَاشِيَةِ The Enveloper

In the name of Allah, Most Compassionate, Most Merciful.	بِسْمِ اللهِ الرَّحْمٰنِ الرَّحِيمِ
1. Did the tidings of the enveloping one reach you?[1]	هَلْ أَتَىٰكَ حَدِيثُ الْغَاشِيَةِ ۝
2. Many faces will be humiliated that Day.	وُجُوهٌ يَوْمَئِذٍ خَاشِعَةٌ ۝
3. Those who worked and were exhausted.[2]	عَامِلَةٌ نَّاصِبَةٌ ۝
4. They will roast in blazing Fire.	تَصْلَىٰ نَارًا حَامِيَةً ۝
5. They will be offered drink from the boiling spring.[3]	تُسْقَىٰ مِنْ عَيْنٍ ءَانِيَةٍ ۝

1 – This Message is worth hearing. *Al-Ghāshiyah* signifies the Last Day which will overtake everyone. It will affect everyone in the broadest sense of the term.

2 – The unbelievers will appear emaciated in view of their ongoing sufferings and hardships. According to some, reference is made to their condition in this life. There are many who exert themselves in this life. However, their hard work will go to waste in that it is not directed towards Truth. They will, thus, suffer in both worlds. Almost the same point is made in verse 11 of *Sūrah al-Hajj*. Shāh 'Abdul Qādir points out that the unbelievers strive hard in this life. However, their efforts will not be acceptable to Allah.

3 – As the Hellfire will render them thirsty, they will cry for a drop of water, thinking that it will comfort them. They will be offered boiling water, and as they take it, it will scald their lips. Once it reaches their insides, it will cut their entrails into pieces, but these will be restored instantly so that they continuously suffer. May Allah protect us against this.

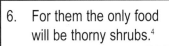

6. For them the only food will be thorny shrubs.[4]	لَّيْسَ لَهُمْ طَعَامٌ إِلَّا مِن ضَرِيعٍ ۝
7. It will neither nourish them nor satisfy their hunger.[5]	لَّا يُسْمِنُ وَلَا يُغْنِى مِن جُوعٍ ۝
8. Many faces will be delighted that Day.	وُجُوهٌ يَوْمَئِذٍ نَّاعِمَةٌ ۝
9. They will be pleased with their deeds.[6]	لِّسَعْيِهَا رَاضِيَةٌ ۝
10. They will be in the High Gardens.	فِى جَنَّةٍ عَالِيَةٍ ۝
11. They will not hear any vanity there.[7]	لَّا تَسْمَعُ فِيهَا لَاغِيَةً ۝
12. Therein is a flowing spring.[8]	فِيهَا عَيْنٌ جَارِيَةٌ ۝

4 – Ḍarīʿ is a thorny bush in Hell. It is known for its bitter taste and stench, which will be more foul than carrion. It will be as hot as Hellfire. When the inmates of Hell ask for food in their starvation, they will be served hot ḍarīʿ.

5 – One takes food for enjoyment, and to support and sustain one's body. Neither of these objectives will be attained when the unbelievers consume ḍarīʿ. It is evident from the above account that it does not offer any pleasure. That it will not satisfy hunger is clearly stated in this verse. In sum, the unbelievers will not enjoy any food or pleasure in Hell. This account is followed by a description of the dwellers of Paradise.

6 – The Believers will rejoice in the fact that their efforts have been appreciated and that they have been rewarded generously for their conduct.

7 – They will not hear anything vain. Obviously, any abuse or indecency is out of the question in the context of Paradise.

8 – The reference is made to a special spring. Some scholars hold that there will be many such springs there.

13. Therein are high couches.	فِيهَا سُرُرٌ مَّرْفُوعَةٌ ﴿١٣﴾
14. And the well-arranged cups.[9]	وَأَكْوَابٌ مَّوْضُوعَةٌ ﴿١٤﴾
15. And the carpets well laid out.[10]	وَنَمَارِقُ مَصْفُوفَةٌ ﴿١٥﴾
16. And the sheets of brocade.[11]	وَزَرَابِيُّ مَبْثُوثَةٌ ﴿١٦﴾
17. Do they not look at the camels,	أَفَلَا يَنظُرُونَ إِلَى ٱلْإِبِلِ
How they are created?[12]	كَيْفَ خُلِقَتْ ﴿١٧﴾
18. And at the sky, how it is raised?[13]	وَإِلَى ٱلسَّمَاءِ كَيْفَ رُفِعَتْ ﴿١٨﴾
19. And at the mountains, how these are rooted?[14]	وَإِلَى ٱلْجِبَالِ كَيْفَ نُصِبَتْ ﴿١٩﴾
20. And at the earth, how it is spread out?[15]	وَإِلَى ٱلْأَرْضِ كَيْفَ سُطِحَتْ ﴿٢٠﴾

9 – Whenever they wish, they will have this to drink.

10 – Reference is made to the well-laid out carpets and couches.

11 – They will be free to take rest as and when they want it. They will not even have to bother about going from one place to another.

12 – Both in their appearance and properties, they are special. See a detailed note on this in *Tafsīr ʿAzīzī*.

13 – That is without any pillar or support.

14 – They do not move even slightly.

15 – Notwithstanding its outward appearance, the earth is level. It has greatly facilitated man to live on it. This was on account of the Signs in nature. It is intriguing that notwithstanding his observation of these wonderful Signs, man does not recognise Divine Power

21. So admonish. Your job is to admonish.	فَذَكِّرْ إِنَّمَا أَنتَ مُذَكِّرٌ ۞
22. You are not a custodian over them.[16]	لَّسْتَ عَلَيْهِم بِمُصَيْطِرٍ ۞
23. Whoever turns away and disbelieves.	إِلَّا مَن تَوَلَّىٰ وَكَفَرَ ۞
24. Such will be punished by Allah with a great punishment.	فَيُعَذِّبُهُ ٱللَّهُ ٱلْعَذَابَ ٱلْأَكْبَرَ ۞
25. To Us is their return.	إِنَّ إِلَيْنَا إِيَابَهُمْ ۞
26. Then it is for Us to take them to account.[17]	ثُمَّ إِنَّ عَلَيْنَا حِسَابَهُم ۞

and Wisdom. This points to the Hereafter and to the wonderful arrangements in the Hereafter. These objects are mentioned specifically, points out Ibn Kathīr, in that the Arabs often pass through forests and deserts. They regularly watch these objects: the camel to ride, the sky above them, the earth below them and the mountains around them. The Qur'ān, therefore, urges them to reflect upon these four objects in particular.

16 – Since they do not reflect even in the face of these manifest Signs, the Prophet ﷺ should not grieve on their account. He has been sent down for admonishing them and for preaching Truth to them. If they do not take heed, he is not their custodian, who has to force them into accepting Faith and changing their hearts. Allah alone can accomplish this.

17 – Whoever disobeys Allah and rejects His Signs, cannot escape from His terrible punishment in the Hereafter. Everyone is bound to return to Him. Allah will take everyone to task for each and every deed. The Prophet ﷺ should, therefore, keep on performing his duty and refer the case of the unbelievers to Allah.

* * *

In the name of Allah, Most Compassionate, Most Merciful.

1. By the dawn. وَالْفَجْرِ ۱

2. And the ten nights. وَلَيَالٍ عَشْرٍ ۲

3. And the even and the odd. وَالشَّفْعِ وَالْوَتْرِ ۳

4. And that night wherein (he) journeys.[1] وَالَّيْلِ إِذَا يَسْرِ ۴

---

1 – Shāh ʿAbdul Qādir states: "By the dawn of ʿĪd al-Aḍḥā during which Ḥajj is performed and the ten nights which precede it and by the even and the odd, i.e. last ten days of Ramaḍān and by the night on which the Prophet journeyed on *miʿrāj*." An oath is taken with reference to these happenings. Most Qurʾānic scholars interpret verse 4 of this *Sūrah* in the sense of the passage of night or when its darkness spreads. In other words, it contrasts with dawn. Another contrasting oath is that of odd and even numbers. Verse 2 of this *Sūrah* might specifically mean ten nights. It is common knowledge that the first ten nights of a month are bright and these gradually tend to turn darker. As for the ten nights falling in the middle of the month, these are both dark and bright. This detailed reference to contrasting things brings home the point that man should not be content with his present condition, be it prosperity or adversity. Nor should he think that his condition will never change. Let man remember that Allah causes contrast and He brings about the same in numerous objects of nature. By the same token, man's condition also undergoes change. This point is illustrated by certain events related in the following verses.

5. This is the oath for men of understanding.[2]	هَلْ فِى ذَلِكَ قَسَمٌ لِّذِى حِجْرٍ ﴿٥﴾
6. Did you see how your Lord treated ʿĀd?	أَلَمْ تَرَ كَيْفَ فَعَلَ رَبُّكَ بِعَادٍ ﴿٦﴾
7. Those of Iram[3] with large pillars.[4]	إِرَمَ ذَاتِ ٱلْعِمَادِ ﴿٧﴾
8. What they had built was something unrivalled in all the lands.[5]	ٱلَّتِى لَمْ يُخْلَقْ مِثْلُهَا فِى ٱلْبِلَـٰدِ ﴿٨﴾
9. And Thamūd who hewed out rocks in the valleys.[6]	وَثَمُودَ ٱلَّذِينَ جَابُوا۟ ٱلصَّخْرَ بِٱلْوَادِ ﴿٩﴾

As to the two *Aḥādīth* in relation to the interpretation of this verse on the authority of Jābir and ʿImrān respectively, Ibn Kathīr prefers the former.

2 – These oaths are not to be taken lightly. Rather, they are grand in every sense of the term. Those gifted with understanding realise that they are marked by a grandeur which reinforces the point under discussion.

3 – ʿĀd was the name of the ancestors after whom ʿĀd's community came to be known. One of his forefathers was Iram. Reference to the latter perhaps signifies that the allusion is to the first generation of ʿĀd, not the subsequent ones. Some maintain that the royal family of the ʿĀd was known as Iram. And Allah knows best.

4 – They built huge structures supported by columns and pillars. Alternatively, this may mean that they enjoyed life walking about on the land, staying in tents erected on pillars. Other scholars opine that the allusion is to their imposing stature. They were as huge in size as pillars are. And Allah knows best.

5 – No other community excelled them in strength. Likewise, their buildings were not matched by any other.

6 – Wādi al-Qurā was the place where they hewed houses out of mountains. Needless to say, these houses were very strong and firm.

10. And Pharaoh, owner of the pegs.[7]	وَفِرْعَوْنَ ذِى ٱلْأَوْتَادِ ﴿١٠﴾
11. They were the ones who transgressed in the lands.	ٱلَّذِينَ طَغَوْا۟ فِى ٱلْبِلَـٰدِ ﴿١١﴾
12. They spread corruption in these.	فَأَكْثَرُوا۟ فِيهَا ٱلْفَسَادَ ﴿١٢﴾
13. Then your Lord let loose on them	فَصَبَّ عَلَيْهِمْ رَبُّكَ
A scourge of suffering.[8]	سَوْطَ عَذَابٍ ﴿١٣﴾
14. Verily your Lord is in ambush.[9]	إِنَّ رَبَّكَ لَبِٱلْمِرْصَادِ ﴿١٤﴾

7 – He had a vast army, hence, he had a large supply of tent pegs. Alternatively, he persecuted his enemies by inserting tiny pegs under their fingernails.

8 – These communities, intoxicated as they were with wealth and authority, caused much mischief. They indulged in misdeeds and rose in rebellion. They thought they were not accountable to anyone and that they would abide forever in this world. It did not occur to them that they would be held accountable for their wrongdoing and rebellion. As they exceeded all limits and their respite was over, Divine punishment befell them suddenly. All strength and expertise was reduced to nothing; their abundant resources could not avail them in any degree.

9 – A person lying in ambush maintains a vigil on his victim's movements. He takes all the relevant factors into account before his assault. By the same token, Allah watches each and every deed of every human being while man cannot see Him. No action is hidden from Him. However, Allah does not punish instantly. Those negligent of Him think that they will not have to answer for their conduct and that they are free to do whatever they want. However, Allah will expose them at the appointed hour. He will recompense

15. So man when he is tested by his Lord	فَأَمَّا ٱلْإِنسَٰنُ إِذَا مَا ٱبْتَلَىٰهُ رَبُّهُۥ
And honoured and bestowed with bounties,	فَأَكْرَمَهُۥ وَنَعَّمَهُۥ
He says: "My Lord has honoured me."[10]	فَيَقُولُ رَبِّىٓ أَكْرَمَنِ ﴿١٥﴾
16. And when He tests man	وَأَمَّآ إِذَا مَا ٱبْتَلَىٰهُ
And straitens his sustenance,	فَقَدَرَ عَلَيْهِ رِزْقَهُۥ
He says: "My Lord has humiliated me."[11]	فَيَقُولُ رَبِّىٓ أَهَٰنَنِ ﴿١٦﴾
17. Nay, you do not treat the orphans well.[12]	كَلَّا ۖ بَل لَّا تُكْرِمُونَ ٱلْيَتِيمَ ﴿١٧﴾

everyone in accordance with his record of deeds. It is then that man will realise that he had been granted a respite and that he was under trial. Allah rewards those who are not misled by their temporary stay in the world and who do not forget the Hereafter.

10 – Believers will be elevated in rank in that they deserve it.

11 – The reference here is to the unbeliever who sets his eye only on this worldly life. For him, adversity or prosperity in this life is the pointer to his honour or disgrace. He fails to recognise that his condition, whatever it is, represents his trial. When he is blessed with bounties, he is tested as to whether he acts gratefully towards Allah. Likewise, when he is afflicted with adversity, his perseverance is ascertained. One's prosperity in this life is not an indication of one's exalted status in the Hereafter. Likewise, one's hard times in the present life do not point to his ultimate disgrace. However, man fails to look at his deeds. Rather, he blames Allah for his plight in brazen fashion.

12 – The unbelievers will not be elevated, for they treated the poor and needy orphans badly.

18. Nor do you exhort

One another to feed
the needy.[13]

وَلَا تَحَـٰٓضُّونَ
عَلَىٰ طَعَامِ ٱلْمِسْكِينِ ۝

19. And you devour the
inheritance greedily.[14]

وَتَأْكُلُونَ ٱلتُّرَاثَ أَكْلًا لَّمًّا ۝

20. And you love
wealth much.[15]

وَتُحِبُّونَ ٱلْمَالَ حُبًّا جَمًّا ۝

21. Nay, When the earth is
disintegrated into pieces.[16]

كَلَّآ إِذَا دُكَّتِ ٱلْأَرْضُ دَكًّا دَكًّا ۝

22. And your Lord appears,[17]

وَجَآءَ رَبُّكَ

And the angels
come in ranks.[18]

وَٱلْمَلَكُ صَفًّا صَفًّا ۝

13 – Far from helping the needy, the unbelievers did not even ask others to look after the poor.

14 – They were guilty of neglecting the Divine Law of inheritance. Without any concern for the lawful or the unlawful they take whatever they can. So doing, they neglect and abuse the rights of orphans and the poor.

15 – The root cause of their error is their lust for wealth. They are interested only in amassing wealth, no matter by what means. Then they do not spend even a single penny on charity. Once again they behave without realising its fatal consequences. Only the unbelievers deify money in that they focus all their energy on amassing it.

16 – All the mountains will be disintegrated and the earth levelled.

17 – Allah's refulgence will be full of glory, as befits Him.

18 – The angels will appear there in order to arrange for the Great Reckoning.

23. And Hell will be brought near that Day.[19]	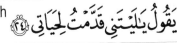
That Day man will reflect.	
However, this reflection will not avail him.[20]	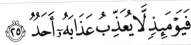
24. He will say: "I wish I had sent forth something (good) in my life."[21]	يَقُولُ يَٰلَيۡتَنِي قَدَّمۡتُ لِحَيَاتِي ٢٤
25. That Day none can punish as He will punish.	فَيَوۡمَئِذٍ لَّا يُعَذِّبُ عَذَابَهُۥٓ أَحَدٌ ٢٥
26. And none can bind as He will bind.[22]	وَلَا يُوثِقُ وَثَاقَهُۥٓ أَحَدٌ ٢٦

19 – Millions of angels will bring out Hell drawing it from its place in front of the Grand Assembly.

20 – The unbelievers will realise then that they were in error. This late realisation will not, however, be of any avail. One's opportunity is limited to this lifetime. One cannot accomplish anything in the Hereafter.

21 – The unbelievers will regret that they did not do anything good which would have helped them in the Next Life. They will deeply regret the absence of any good deed on their part. Had they done good, it would have availed them.

22 – Allah will severely punish the wicked on the Day. They will be subject to such a harsh punishment which cannot be even imagined. Shāh 'Abdul 'Azīz elaborates upon this thus: "All the modes of punishment such as punishing by fire, biting by snakes or scorpions in Hell will be much more severe than one can imagine. This constitutes physical punishment. As for their emotional punishment, Allah will make them remorseful. As it is, emotional pain is more agonising than physical pain. Then the inmates of Hell will be tied in fetters around their necks and feet. All the gates of Hell will be

27. O the peaceful soul.	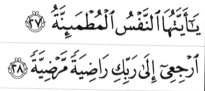
28. Return to your Lord, well–pleased and well-pleasing.	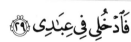
29. Enter the ranks of My pious servants.	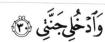
30. And enter My Garden.[23]	وَٱدۡخُلِى جَنَّتِى ۝

sealed. However, they will be tormented by their own guilty conscience. While being imprisoned, one thinks hard and long. Allah will afflict the unbelievers with this chastisement as well. Such emotional torment is more painful than corporal imprisonment. It is common knowledge that the insane hate going out, apprehending some danger. Even scenic beauty does not soothe them."

23 – The account of the wicked is contrasted here with that of those who derived pleasure from remembering Allah and obeying Him. On the Day of Judgement, they will be told: "O satisfied soul! You were devoted to your Lord. Now go ahead in peace and delight towards a high place, free from all apprehension. Be among the select servants of Allah and abide in His magnificent Paradise." According to some reports, this Glad Tidings is announced to True Believers when they are about to die. It emerges from the life of spiritual masters that they enjoy a similar tranquillity even amid the turmoil of the present life: "O our Lord! We seek from You the satisfied soul which is pleased with Your sight and is reconciled to Your decree and is content with obeying You."

We have defined the *Muṭma'innah*, *Ammārah* and *Lawwāmah* souls in the opening part of our commentary on *Sūrah al-Qiyāmah*.

***

Al-Balad	سُوْرَةُ الْبَلَدِ	*The City*

In the name of Allah, Most Compassionate, Most Merciful.

بِسْمِ اللَّهِ الرَّحْمَنِ الرَّحِيمِ

1. I swear by this city.[1]

لَا أُقْسِمُ بِهَذَا الْبَلَدِ ۝

2. And for you there will be no restriction in this city.[2]

وَأَنتَ حِلٌّ بِهَذَا الْبَلَدِ ۝

3. And by the one who bears and what it bears.[3]

وَوَالِدٍ وَمَا وَلَدَ ۝

1 – The oath refers to Makkah.

2 – It is forbidden to fight within Makkah. This prohibition was, however, lifted as an exception for the Prophet ﷺ on the day of the conquest of Makkah. Whoever took on the Prophet ﷺ that day was put to death. Some wicked people were killed while they were near the walls of the Kaʿbah. However, the same prohibition has been in force since that day and will continue so till the Day of Judgement. The invocation to Makkah in this verse underlies the hardships man has to undergo. The most outstanding human being of all times was subject to persecution and suffering in Makkah at the hands of his enemies. He is comforted, told the prophecy that though he is not held in esteem presently, he will soon enter the same town as the victor. Furthermore, he will have Divine leave to cleanse the place for all times and to punish the guilty. This Qurʾānic prediction came true in 8 A.H.

Some interpret verse 2 of this *Sūrah* in the sense of Makkah as the birthplace and town of the Prophet ﷺ.

3 – That is Adam and his progeny.

4.	Verily We have created man in hardship.[4]	لَقَدْ خَلَقْنَا الْإِنسَٰنَ فِى كَبَدٍ ﴿٤﴾
5.	Does he think no one can overpower him?[5]	أَيَحْسَبُ أَن لَّن يَقْدِرَ عَلَيْهِ أَحَدٌ ﴿٥﴾
6.	He says: "I have spent plenty of wealth."[6]	يَقُولُ أَهْلَكْتُ مَالًا لُّبَدًا ﴿٦﴾
7.	Does he think no one watches him?[7]	أَيَحْسَبُ أَن لَّمْ يَرَهُۥٓ أَحَدٌ ﴿٧﴾

4 – Man is subject to much hardship. He is afflicted with disease, grief and many other worries. Hardly does a moment pass when man is absolutely carefree. Actually man has been created in a way that he cannot be free from worries at any point of time. This truth is evident if one observes men's lives. The Prophet ﷺ, the best of human beings, underwent intense persecution and suffering in Makkah. This point is further elaborated upon in verse 4 of this *Sūrah*.

5 – As man passes through many hardships, it should make him all the more humble. He should realise his total dependence upon the Divine decree and pledge his complete obedience to Allah. He should become all the more conscious of his needs. However, man is mostly oblivious of these Truths. For he thinks that no one can outdo or punish him for his rebellion.

6 – The unbelievers regarded opposition to the Prophet ﷺ and Islam as a virtue and wasted their money on evil deeds. They took great pride in spending plenty of money on misdeeds. They thought no one could subdue them. However, soon they will recognise that all their wealth has been wasted; rather, it will entail a terrible punishment for them.

7 – Allah watches everything. He knows the intention which prompts one to spend money. Any boasting on this count is therefore pointless.

8. Have We not blessed him with two eyes?[8]	أَلَمْ نَجْعَل لَّهُ عَيْنَيْنِ ﴿٨﴾
9. And with a tongue and two lips.[9]	وَلِسَانًا وَشَفَتَيْنِ ﴿٩﴾
10. And We have shown him the two passes.[10]	وَهَدَيْنَاهُ النَّجْدَيْنِ ﴿١٠﴾
11. Yet he does not attempt the obstacle.[11]	فَلَا اقْتَحَمَ الْعَقَبَةَ ﴿١١﴾
12. And what do you think the obstacle is?	وَمَا أَدْرَاكَ مَا الْعَقَبَةُ ﴿١٢﴾
13. Freeing the neck.[12]	فَكُّ رَقَبَةٍ ﴿١٣﴾

8 – As Allah has invested man with eyesight, He of course watches over everything which man does. He is All-Seeing.

9 – These facilitate man in conversation and taking food.

10 – Allah has spelled out the way to both Truth and evil. Man should shun evil and pursue good. Man has been provided with an innate inclination for Truth. This point is elaborated upon further by sending down the Messengers.

Some take *Najdayn* as the female breast in the sense that Allah guides the baby in how to take milk and nourish itself.

11 – Notwithstanding the showering of Divine bounties and an elaborate arrangement for Guidance, man still refuses to embrace Faith. Nor does he opt for excellent morals and manners which would elevate him in rank. The cause of Faith is spoken of as the valley in that it calls for some hard work.

12 – That is freeing the slaves or helping those in debt to secure release.

14. Or feeding the hungry in his poverty,[13]	أَوۡ إِطۡعَٰمٌ فِى يَوۡمٍ ذِى مَسۡغَبَةٍ ﴿١٤﴾
15. The orphans who are your kin.[14]	يَتِيمًا ذَا مَقۡرَبَةٍ ﴿١٥﴾
16. Or the needy who are suffering.[15]	أَوۡ مِسۡكِينًا ذَا مَتۡرَبَةٍ ﴿١٦﴾
17. Then be among those who believe[16]	ثُمَّ كَانَ مِنَ ٱلَّذِينَ ءَامَنُوا۟
And exhort patience to one another	وَتَوَاصَوۡا۟ بِٱلصَّبۡرِ
And those who exhort mercy to one another.[17]	وَتَوَاصَوۡا۟ بِٱلۡمَرۡحَمَةِ ﴿١٧﴾
18. Such are the people of great fortune.[18]	أُو۟لَٰٓئِكَ أَصۡحَٰبُ ٱلۡمَيۡمَنَةِ ﴿١٨﴾

13 – Helping famine victims.

14 – Looking after the orphan, treating kith and kin with affection. Whoever does these good deeds is entitled to a double reward.

15 – One should spend money on helping those in abject poverty. Money is not to be wasted on marriage or burial rituals or on such deeds which betray disobedience to Allah. Whoever is guilty of this incurs punishment and disgrace upon himself in both worlds.

16 – Faith should be the moving spirit behind all good deeds. It is the most important prerequisite. Without sincere faith, one's deeds go to waste.

17 – Believers should exhort one another that patience be shown in performing duty. Likewise, mercy should be shown to Allah's creatures so that He may have mercy on us.

18 – Such are indeed blessed who receive their record in their right hand and who are made to stand to the right of the Divine Throne.

19. And those who deny Our Signs,	وَالَّذِينَ كَفَرُوا بِـَايَـٰتِنَا
They are the people of ill fortune.[19]	هُمْ أَصْحَـٰبُ الْمَشْـَمَةِ ۝
20. They will be in the enclosing Fire.[20]	عَلَيْهِمْ نَارٌ مُّؤْصَدَةٌ ۝

19 – Reference is made to those cursed, wicked people who will be handed over their record in their left hand and who will be made to stand to the left of the Throne.

20 – Once all the unbelievers are hurled into Hell, its gates will be sealed. May Allah protect us against it. *Āmeen.*

* * *

| Ash-Shams | سُورَةُ الشَّمْسِ | The Sun |

In the name of Allah, Most Compassionate, Most Merciful.

بِسۡمِ ٱللَّهِ ٱلرَّحۡمَٰنِ ٱلرَّحِيمِ

1. By the sun
   and when it dawns.

وَٱلشَّمۡسِ وَضُحَىٰهَا ﴿١﴾

2. And by the moon
   when it follows the sun.[1]

وَٱلۡقَمَرِ إِذَا تَلَىٰهَا ﴿٢﴾

3. And by the day
   when it turns bright.[2]

وَٱلنَّهَارِ إِذَا جَلَّىٰهَا ﴿٣﴾

4. And by the night
   when it covers it.[3]

وَٱلَّيۡلِ إِذَا يَغۡشَىٰهَا ﴿٤﴾

5. And by the sky
   and Him Who built it.[4]

وَٱلسَّمَآءِ وَمَا بَنَىٰهَا ﴿٥﴾

6. And by the earth
   and Him Who spread out.[5]

وَٱلۡأَرۡضِ وَمَا طَحَىٰهَا ﴿٦﴾

1 – The moonlight which spreads after sunset.

2 – The bright morning when sunlight appears sharply.

3 – The reference here is to the darkness of night when no sunlight is visible.

4 – Reference is made either to the glory of the sky or to that of its Creator.

5 – Allah has spread out in His wisdom the earth, enabling man to settle on it. Some scholars take this to mean a reference to the Creator Himself.

7. And by the soul and Him Who has proportioned it.[6]	وَنَفْسٍ وَمَا سَوَّىٰهَا ۝
8. Then inspired it with knowledge of wickedness and piety.[7]	فَأَلْهَمَهَا فُجُورَهَا وَتَقْوَىٰهَا ۝
9. Whoever purifies it attains salvation.[8]	قَدْ أَفْلَحَ مَن زَكَّىٰهَا ۝
10. And whoever disregards it is unsuccessful.[9]	وَقَدْ خَابَ مَن دَسَّىٰهَا ۝

6 – Allah has provided man with balanced temperament, sense perception, limbs and faculties of all sorts. Moreover, Allah has made it possible for man to follow good or evil.

7 – Allah has granted man the faculty to follow the dictates of nature and reason in order to distinguish between good and evil. The same guidance has been clearly spelled out by the Messengers. Through their detailed teachings they have shown the way to both good and evil. It is Allah Who is the Creator of man's heart. One is free to opt for the way of good or the way of evil. While angels direct man to good, Satan misleads man into committing evil. In the final analysis, however, Allah is the Creator of everything. Therefore all good and evil is ascribed to Him. This is a complex issue which has baffled many. May Allah grant us the ability to appreciate this point well.

8 – Purging the self consists in subjecting one's physical and sexual power to the control of reason, which in turn, should be bound to the *Sharī'ah*. This will illuminate one's soul and heart with Divine Light.

9 – The unbelievers are guilty of letting themselves go absolutely loose and free. They have no concern whatsoever with reason or the *Sharī'ah*. They are devotees of their own selfish desires. Those guilty of this behaviour are worse than animals. Verses 9 and 10 of this *Sūrah* constitute a response to the oath in the following sense: just as Allah has contrasted the sunlight with moonlight, bright day with

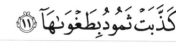
11. Thamud rejected it
as false out of their rebellion.[10]

كَذَّبَتْ ثَمُودُ بِطَغْوَىٰهَآ ﴿١١﴾

12. When the most wretched
of them stood up.[11]

إِذِ ٱنۢبَعَثَ أَشْقَىٰهَا ﴿١٢﴾

13. Allah's Messenger told them:

فَقَالَ لَهُمْ رَسُولُ ٱللَّهِ

"Beware! This is the she-camel of Allah.
It is her turn of drinking water." [12]

نَاقَةَ ٱللَّهِ وَسُقْيَٰهَا ﴿١٣﴾

14. They rejected it as false
and hamstrung her.

فَكَذَّبُوهُ فَعَقَرُوهَا

Then their Lord inflicted
on them the punishment

فَدَمْدَمَ عَلَيْهِمْ رَبُّهُم

For their sins and
levelled them.[13]

بِذَنۢبِهِمْ فَسَوَّىٰهَا ﴿١٤﴾

dark night and the height of the sky with the depth of the earth, the two contrasting powers of good and evil are found in the human self. He has enabled man to follow either. It is Allah Who will pronounce Judgement on us all regardless of which way we followed. Creation of good and evil is as essential as that of darkness and light.

10 – They rejected the Prophet ﷺ as false. Verse 10 recounts the story which serves as a lesson. In its detail, the story features in *Sūrah al-Aʻrāf*.

11 – This accursed person was Qadhār ibn Sālif.

12 – They were warned not to do any harm to the she-camel or disrupt its water supply. The latter is mentioned in particular, for they had been prompted to kill her on account of the same. It is referred to as Allah's she-camel in that Allah presented it as a Sign confirming the Prophet Ṣāliḥ's messengership. He made it binding upon people to treat her well. This story appears in detail in *Sūrah al-Aʻrāf*.

13 – The Prophet Ṣāliḥ ﷺ warned his community not to harm the she-camel (*Sūrah al-Aʻrāf*: 73). If they did, they would be subject to a

15. And He did not fear its consequences.[14]	وَلَا يَخَافُ عُقۡبَٰهَا ۝

terrible punishment. However, his community did not take his warning seriously. They rejected the Prophet ﷺ as false and hamstrung the she-camel. Ultimately, what the Prophet Ṣāliḥ ﷺ had warned came true. Allah obliterated the whole community.

14 – Earthly kings might fear some trouble or rebellion in a part of their kingdom. Allah does not and cannot entertain any such apprehension. For there is no one to rise against Him or to restrain Him from punishing the wicked.

* * *

Al-Layl	سُوْرَةُ الَّيْلِ	*The Night*

In the name of Allah, Most Compassionate, Most Merciful.

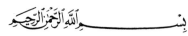

1. By the night when it spreads.

وَالَّيْلِ إِذَا يَغْشَى ۝

2. And by the Day when it brightens.

وَالنَّهَارِ إِذَا تَجَلَّى ۝

3. And by that which He has created male and female.

وَمَا خَلَقَ الذَّكَرَ وَالْأُنْثَى ۝

4. Your deeds are various.¹

إِنَّ سَعْيَكُمْ لَشَتَّى ۝

5. So one who gives and is God-conscious.

فَأَمَّا مَنْ أَعْطَى وَاتَّقَى ۝

6. And testifies to good.

وَصَدَّقَ بِالْحُسْنَى ۝

7. For him We will facilitate an easy path.²

فَسَنُيَسِّرُهُ لِلْيُسْرَى ۝

8. And whoever acts miserly and is indifferent.

وَأَمَّا مَنْ بَخِلَ وَاسْتَغْنَى ۝

1 – As the universe is characterised by contrasting objects such as day and night, male and female, man's deeds too, have different bearings. Given this, these engender different consequences, a point elaborated in the following verses.

2 – Whoever spends his money in a good cause and fears Allah, firmly believes in Islam and the Tidings announced by Allah is enabled, in accordance with Divine Law, to do good. He will eventually be admitted to Paradise which embodies every conceivable comfort and joy.

9.	And rejects good as false.	وَكَذَّبَ بِٱلْحُسْنَىٰ ﴿٩﴾
10.	We will lead him to hardship[3]	فَسَنُيَسِّرُهُۥ لِلْعُسْرَىٰ ﴿١٠﴾
11.	His wealth will not avail him when he perishes.[4]	وَمَا يُغْنِى عَنْهُ مَالُهُۥٓ إِذَا تَرَدَّىٰٓ ﴿١١﴾
12.	It is for Us to guide.	إِنَّ عَلَيْنَا لَلْهُدَىٰ ﴿١٢﴾
13.	And with Us is both the Hereafter and this world.[5]	وَإِنَّ لَنَا لَلْءَاخِرَةَ وَٱلْأُولَىٰ ﴿١٣﴾
14.	So I have warned you of the blazing Fire.[6]	فَأَنذَرْتُكُمْ نَارًا تَلَظَّىٰ ﴿١٤﴾
15.	Only the wretched will be consigned to it.	لَا يَصْلَىٰهَآ إِلَّا ٱلْأَشْقَى ﴿١٥﴾

3 – Whoever does not spend in Allah's way, does not care about His pleasure and the reward of the Hereafter, rejects Islam and Divine teachings as false, his heart is gradually constricted, rendering him unable to do any good. Eventually, he will be gripped by Divine wrath. This is Allah's way when good and evil follow their respective ways, He facilitates its pursuit for them. For man is free to choose the path he selects. Almost the same point comes out of verse 20 of *Sūrah Banī Isrā'īl*.

4 – Reference is made to those who wax proud about their wealth and who are indifferent to the Hereafter. Their wealth will not, however, avail them against Divine punishment.

5 – It is not Divine Will to compel one into doing good or evil. Allah nonetheless arranges for guidance and spells out what is good and what is evil. He has explained it all very clearly. Hence, one will be recompensed in accordance with one's conduct.

6 – Reference is made to the blazing Hellfire reserved exclusively for the worst of criminals and wicked people.

16. One who rejects it as false and turns away.[7]	اَلَّذِى كَذَّبَ وَتَوَلَّىٰ ۝
17. And We will deliver the righteous from it.[8]	وَسَيُجَنَّبُهَا الْأَتْقَى ۝
18. He who spends his wealth in order to purify himself.[9]	اَلَّذِى يُؤْتِى مَالَهُ يَتَزَكَّىٰ ۝
19. And who has no favour from anyone to pay back.	وَمَا لِأَحَدٍ عِنْدَهُ مِنْ نِعْمَةٍ تُجْزَىٰ ۝
20. But only seeks the pleasure of his Lord, Most High.	إِلَّا ابْتِغَاءَ وَجْهِ رَبِّهِ الْأَعْلَى ۝
21. And he will soon be well pleased.[10]	وَلَسَوْفَ يَرْضَىٰ ۝

7 – He will be consigned to Hell forever. He will never get out of it.

8 – The pious will be saved from Hell.

9 – The objective is to protect the soul against evil conduct. The pious are not prompted by any hypocrisy in doing good.

10 – Their spending in charity does not amount to doing good for someone. They do it only for winning Allah's pleasure. For the sake of Divine vision they are prepared to sacrifice everything which they have. Such are destined for a happy end. All their wishes will be fulfilled. This point also occurs in verse 120 of *Sūrah at-Tawbah*.

Although the message of these verses has universal import, it emerges from several authentic reports that these verses were sent down as a tribute to Abū Bakr Ṣiddīq ﷺ. It, no doubt, constitutes his great excellence. One can imagine his good fortune in that the Qur'ān itself speaks of him as a pious person. The Qur'ānic norm about piety is stated in verse 13 of *Sūrah al-Ḥujurāt*. In verse 21 of this *Sūrah*, it is clearly mentioned that Allah is well-pleased with Abū Bakr. It is a pointer to the Great Tidings about the Prophet ﷺ himself in *Sūrah aḍ-Ḍuḥā*.

* * *

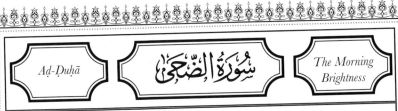

| | Ad-Ḍuḥā | سُوْرَةُ الضُّحٰى | The Morning Brightness |

| In the name of Allah, Most Compassionate, Most Merciful. |  |

1. By the morning brightness.

وَالضُّحٰى ۞

2. And by the night when it overtakes.

وَالَّيْلِ إِذَا سَجٰى ۞

3. Your Lord has not abandoned you. Nor is He displeased.[1]

مَا وَدَّعَكَ رَبُّكَ وَمَا قَلٰى ۞

1 – According to authentic reports, Gabriel عليه السلام did not bring any Revelation for a long time to the Prophet ﷺ. Observing this, the Makkan polytheists took to saying: "Muḥammad has been abandoned by his Lord." As a rejoinder, these verses were sent down. In our opinion this break in Revelations is similar to the break taken after the opening verses of *Sūrah al-'Alaq*. The Prophet ﷺ was much distressed during this period. He was finally comforted by the angel: as O *al-Muddaththir* [*Sūrah* 74:1]. It is likely that the Prophet's opponents had taken to making such remarks during this period. This point is corroborated by Ibn Kathīr on the authority of Muḥammad Ibn Isḥāq. It is also likely that the following event happened during the same period which is recorded in authentic *Ḥadīth*. Once the Prophet ﷺ could not rise from his bed owing to illness. A wicked woman took to saying: "O Muḥammad! It appears that your devil has forsaken you." All these baseless notions are dispelled in this *Sūrah*. An oath is taken by the bright morning and by the dark night. This is followed by the assertion that all the notions of the Prophet's enemies are absolutely false. For Allah is not displeased with him. Nor has He forsaken him. As He produces numerous Signs manifesting His power and glory, such as the alternation of day and night, the same holds true for the inward

4.	The Hereafter is better for you than the present life.[2]	وَلَلْأَخِرَةُ خَيْرٌ لَّكَ مِنَ الْأُولَىٰ ٤
5.	And your Lord will grant you soon	وَلَسَوْفَ يُعْطِيكَ رَبُّكَ
	That which will please you.[3]	فَتَرْضَىٰ ٥
6.	Did He not find you as an orphan and provide for you?[4]	أَلَمْ يَجِدْكَ يَتِيمًا فَآوَىٰ ٦

condition. That night overtakes a bright day does not indicate any displeasure on Allah's part nor does it signify perpetual darkness. By the same token, a temporary break in Revelation cannot be taken as indicative of Allah's displeasure towards His Messenger. Nor does it imply that Revelation had stopped once and for all. Such a notion amounts to questioning Allah's Absolute Power, Wisdom and Knowledge. For it would imply that He did not know what kind of person He had chosen for the messengership. May Allah defend us against entertaining such notions.

2 – Each phase of the Prophet's career was better than the previous one. The temporary stoppage of Revelation does not point to any decline in his status. Rather, it serves as the means for his exaltation and elevation. As for the last phase in his career, the whole of mankind will rally round him on the Day of Judgement. The favours to be showered upon him in the Next Life are certainly much better than the ones conferred upon him in this life.

3 – Far from any displeasure, Allah will bestow upon him so many favours and bounties which will please him fully. It is stated in *Hadīth* literature that the Prophet ﷺ said: "I would not be pleased until each and every member of my community is released from Hell."

4 – The Prophet's father died before his birth. While the Prophet ﷺ was only six years old, his mother passed away. Up to the age of eight years, he was under the care of his grandfather, 'Abd al-Muṭṭalib. Then the privilege of looking after him fell to his uncle,

7. And found you in error and guided you?[5]	وَوَجَدَكَ ضَالًّا فَهَدَىٰ ۝
8. And found you resourceless and made you self-sufficient?[6]	وَوَجَدَكَ عَائِلًا فَأَغْنَىٰ ۝

Abū Ṭālib. The latter spent his whole life in helping, supporting and defending him. However, Abū Ṭālib too died, a little before the Prophet's emigration. Then the Prophet ﷺ moved to Madinah, to be helped by the Anṣār. This indeed blessed the Aws and Khazraj tribes of Madinah. It must be said to their credit that they discharged the duty well and in an unprecedented manner. All these types of protection for the Prophet ﷺ were a direct result of the Divine care taken for him. This point is made by Ibn Kathīr.

5 – As the Prophet ﷺ grew as a youth, he developed a strong distaste for the polytheistic beliefs and practices of his community. For he was devoted exclusively to the worship of the One True God. His link with Allah was very strong. He had been invested with a remarkable capacity for guiding mankind and turning to Allah. However, he could not find a way of expressing and articulating his quest for Truth. Essentially, he looked for a straight way to Truth. He would retire to mountains and caves and dedicate himself to worshipping and invoking Allah. Eventually, Allah directed the Archangel Gabriel عليه السلام to visit him in Ḥirā' Cave. Gabriel عليه السلام brought to him Divine Revelation and instructed him in Truth and in guiding his fellow human beings. The Qur'ān was gradually sent down to him, a point also made in verse 52 of *Surah ash-Shūrā*. As for the interpretation of the Qur'ānic expression *Ḍalla* employed in this verse, one should refer to our note on verse 95 of *Surah Yūsuf*.

6 – The Prophet ﷺ became Khadījah's business partner and earned rich dividends. Then she married him and placed all her wealth at his disposal. This points to his apparent affluence. As for his inner and spiritual affluence, Allah alone knows it best. It is simply beyond anyone else to imagine it. The point pressed home is that the Prophet ﷺ was a recipient of Divine Blessings from the very beginning and he would continue to enjoy the same exalted status

9. So do not oppress the orphans.[7]

فَأَمَّا الْيَتِيمَ فَلَا تَقْهَرْ ۝

10. And do not rebuke the beggar.[8]

وَأَمَّا السَّآئِلَ فَلَا تَنْهَرْ ۝

11. And recount the favours of your Lord.[9]

وَأَمَّا بِنِعْمَةِ رَبِّكَ فَحَدِّثْ ۝

in the future. Allah brought him up in a special manner. In light of these facts, it is preposterous to think that Allah would ever forsake him.

7 – The Prophet ﷺ is here directed to take care of the needy and the destitute. For Allah provided him with refuge during his orphan days. One follows Divine teachings in acquiring excellent morals and manners, a point also stated in verse 138 of Sūrah al-Baqarah.

8 – Initially the Prophet ﷺ was resourceless. However, Allah blessed him with opulence. A thankful servant of Allah is not irked by requests made by needy people to help them. He is not supposed to rebuke or disgrace those who seek his assistance. On the contrary, he should treat them kindly and generously. The reports recorded in Ḥadīth literature about the Prophet's exemplary treatment of the poor are even acknowledged by his worst enemies.

According to the author of Rūḥ al-Maʿānī, it is forbidden to rebuke a needy person, if one can excuse oneself gently. However, if the needy person is too persistent and does not listen, one is permitted to rebuke him.

9 – The Sharīʿah prescribes it as a desirable act to mention the favours done by one's benefactor in order to express gratitude. One should not do so out of any boastfulness however. The Prophet ﷺ is, therefore, told here to relate the favours done to him, especially the tremendous favour of guidance, referred to in verse 7 of this Sūrah. Preaching and expounding Truth is his duty. It is probable that the term Ḥadīth, consisting of the Prophet's sayings, originated from the Qurʾānic expression used in verse 11 of this Sūrah.

***

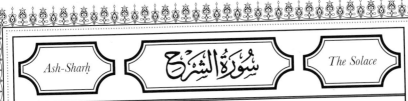

Ash-Sharḥ — The Solace

In the name of Allah, Most Compassionate, Most Merciful.

1. Did We not expand your breast?[1]

2. And relieve you of your burden.

3. What had burdened your back.[2]

---

1 – Allah blessed the Prophet ﷺ with immense knowledge, a remarkable capacity to discharge his office of Messengership and to deal with his enemies. As a result, the Prophet was not daunted by the opposition of such a massive number of detractors.

It is borne out by *Ḥadīth* and *Sīrah* literature that the angels literally opened the Prophet's chest several times. The present verse, however, does not apparently refer to this event. And Allah knows best.

2 – Being a recipient of Revelation was initially hard for the Prophet ﷺ. However, it became easy with the passage of time. Initially, he might have felt the burden of his office, but this was removed. Or the reference may be to such deeds of his which he thought desirable. However, at a later date, these were branded as undesirable or contrary to Divine Wisdom. In such a situation, the Prophet ﷺ must have felt deeply grieved, as is the condition of a sinner. This verse, however, gives him the Glad Tidings that he will not be held accountable for his exercising discretion. This interpretation is offered by some classical authorities.

Shāh 'Abdul 'Azīz holds: "The Prophet's innate capacity and quest for Truth called for reaching such heights with his heart, that owing to its lack of proper training he found it hard to cope with.

4. And exalted your fame.[3]

وَرَفَعْنَا لَكَ ذِكْرَكَ ﴿٤﴾

5. So there is ease
   along with hardship.

فَإِنَّ مَعَ الْعُسْرِ يُسْرًا ﴿٥﴾

6. There is hardship
   with ease.[4]

إِنَّ مَعَ الْعُسْرِ يُسْرًا ﴿٦﴾

Allah, however, opened his breast and enabled him to take everything in his stride. As a result, all his problems were over, and this relieved him greatly."

3 – All the Messengers and angels held the Prophet ﷺ in high esteem. Likewise, all those endowed with understanding among men speak highly of him. In *Adhān*, *Iqāmah*, the Friday Sermon, the credal statement of Islam and other components of the Prayer, his name immediately follows that of Allah's. Furthermore, whenever Allah asks man in the Qur'ān to obey Him, it also carries the directive that the Prophet ﷺ be obeyed.

4 – Reference is made to the hardships suffered by the Prophet ﷺ in the cause of Allah. Every hardship is accompanied by some ease. For example, his capacity to endure difficulties was increased, enabling him to put up with them. Likewise, his remembrance of Allah inspired him to undertake even the most difficult task. Alternatively, the verse might mean that Allah bestowed spiritual tranquillity upon him. It emerges from this *Sūrah* that one should look forward to relief and comfort. Allah promises that all the problems faced by the Prophet ﷺ will soon be over. This point is reinforced in so far as the statement occurs twice in this *Sūrah*. It is evident from *Hadīth* and *Sīrah* literature that all the problems confronting the Prophet ﷺ were gradually removed. Rather, each hardship was followed by several comforts. Allah's way is still the same. Whoever bears hardships patiently while maintaining a sound, firm conviction in Allah and who dedicates himself fully only to Him can look forward to His Mercy and Grace. One should not despair of Divine Mercy in the face of crisis. Such a person will

| 7. When you are free, devote yourself. | فَإِذَا فَرَغْتَ فَانصَبْ ۝ |
| 8. And turn to your Lord (single-mindedly).[5] | وَإِلَى رَبِّكَ فَارْغَب ۝ |

certainly be blessed by Allah. He will be helped in a variety of ways. This point is elaborated upon further in *Hadīth* literature.

5 – When the Prophet ﷺ finishes preaching to people, he is instructed to retire to his private quarters and engage himself in glorifying and worshipping Allah. This will accrue him further ease and joy. He should turn to his Lord without any distraction.

Preaching the Truth to people and admonishing them was undoubtedly the highest act of worship on the part of the Prophet ﷺ. However, it involved his constant interaction with people. Hence, the verse suggests that he should directly approach his Lord. This verse has been interpreted in a variety of ways. The above commentary, however, seems more plausible.

* * *

At-Tīn	سُوۡرَةُ التِّیۡنِ	The Fig

In the name of Allah, Most Compassionate, Most Merciful.

1.	By the fig and by the olive.[1]	
2.	And by Mount Sinai.	
3.	And by this secure town.[2]	
4.	We have created man in the best mould.[3]	

1 – Both the fig and olive are known for their numerous benefits. Both are mentioned in the context of man's creation. Some scholars, however, contend that at-Tīn and az-Zaitūn stand for the two mountains in the vicinity of Jerusalem. Taken in this sense, the oath is not by these two common fruits. Rather, the reference is to the blessed place where both fruits grow in plenty. This region is also the birthplace of the Prophet Jesus ﷺ.

2 – It was at Mount Sinai that Allah spoke directly to the Prophet Moses ﷺ. The blessed town alludes to Makkah in that Prophet Muḥammad ﷺ, leader of all the Messengers, was sent down there. Likewise, the Qur'ān was revealed there.

3 – All these blessed places having strong associations with outstanding Messengers testify that man has been created in the best mould and been provided with exceptional faculties. If man acts along the desired lines, he may even outdo the angels. Rather, the angels will fall in prostration before him.

5. Then We reduce him to the lowest of the low.[4]	ثُمَّ رَدَدْنَٰهُ أَسْفَلَ سَٰفِلِينَ ٥
6. Except those who believe and do good.	إِلَّا ٱلَّذِينَ ءَامَنُوا۟ وَعَمِلُوا۟ ٱلصَّٰلِحَٰتِ
There is an unending reward for them.[5]	فَلَهُمْ أَجْرٌ غَيْرُ مَمْنُونٍ ٦
7. So what makes you deny the Day of Judgement?[6]	فَمَا يُكَذِّبُكَ بَعْدُ بِٱلدِّينِ ٧

4 – Shāh 'Abdul Qādir observes: "Allah has given this opportunity to man to match the angels. However, if he opts for evil, he ends up as one worse than animals."

5 – Reference is made here to inexhaustible Divine rewards.

6 – The address is to man. In the face of these arguments, there are no grounds whatsoever to deny the doctrine of the Hereafter. If this verse is taken to address the Prophet 🌼, it would mean that he is asked what prompts his enemies to reject him as false. Remember that Allah created man in the best fashion. By temperament man is capable of matching or even excelling the angels, if he devotes himself to goodness and piety. No creature of Allah can outdo man in this respect. Did not perfect specimens of humanity make their appearance in Jerusalem, Mount Sinai and Makkah at different stages of human history? If men follow in their footsteps, they are bound for high rank and abiding success. However, man himself opts for humiliation and disgrace and forfeits his privileged position. Allah does not disgrace any pious person, without reason. On the contrary, He rewards him immensely for even a minor good deed. In the face of these truths, it does not befit anyone to dismiss the doctrine of the Hereafter which is based upon the principle of justice and commonsense. The only possibility in which this doctrine can be rejected is that one regards the whole universe as something without any underlying purpose, without any ruler, without any law governing

| 8. | Is Allah not the greatest of all judges?[7] |  |

its working, which will recompense good and evil. This point is countered by the Qur'ānic assertion that Allah is the Best of those who judge (verse 8 of this *Sūrah*).

7 – As compared to Divine dominion, all worldly authority is pointless. Since even tiny states punish criminals and reward their loyal subjects, it should be believed that Allah being the Best of judges will recompense everyone.

* * *

| Al-ʿAlaq | سُوْرَةُ الْعَلَقِ | The Clot |

In the name of Allah, Most Compassionate, Most Merciful.

بِسْمِ اللَّهِ الرَّحْمَنِ الرَّحِيمِ

1. Read in the name of your Lord[1] Who has created.[2]

اقْرَأْ بِاسْمِ رَبِّكَ الَّذِى خَلَقَ ۝

2. He created man from a clot of blood.[3]

خَلَقَ الْإِنسَـٰنَ مِنْ عَلَقٍ ۝

1 – The first five verses of this *Sūrah* are the earliest Revelation. While the Prophet ﷺ was busy worshipping the One True God in Ḥirāʾ Cave, Gabriel عليه السلام appeared before him suddenly, directing him to recite. When the Prophet ﷺ regretted his inability to recite, the angel seized him several times and repeatedly asked him to recite. The Prophet ﷺ repeated his reply and this exchange happened three times. On the third occasion the angel asked him to recite in the name of his Lord, suggesting that he should recite with the blessings and support of his Lord. Implicit in this is the point that Allah brought the Prophet ﷺ up in a special way. He was asked to carry out an important assignment. Given this, Allah will definitely not forsake him. He will be trained under Divine care, as has been ensured up to this point of time.

2 – Since Allah has created everything, He will enable the Prophet ﷺ to recite.

3 – That is a clot of blood which is devoid of sense perception, feeling and life. It is Allah Who invests man with the faculty of reason. He elevates His select servants to perfection. Therefore, it is logical that He can enable an unlettered person to recite and impart wisdom. It is not at all hard for Him. This point is developed further in the following verse.

3.	Read and your Lord is Most Noble.[4]	اقْرَأْ وَرَبُّكَ ٱلْأَكْرَمُ ﴿٣﴾
4.	He Who has taught by the pen.[5]	ٱلَّذِى عَلَّمَ بِٱلْقَلَمِ ﴿٤﴾
5.	Taught man what he did not know.[6]	عَلَّمَ ٱلْإِنسَـٰنَ مَا لَمْ يَعْلَمْ ﴿٥﴾
6.	Nay, man transgresses.	كَلَّآ إِنَّ ٱلْإِنسَـٰنَ لَيَطْغَىٰٓ ﴿٦﴾
7.	As he considers himself self-sufficient.[7]	أَن رَّءَاهُ ٱسْتَغْنَىٰٓ ﴿٧﴾

4 – The Prophet ﷺ was brought up in a special way. His exceptional qualities were known to everyone. Given this, Allah will certainly bless him. He is the Most Merciful of the Merciful. Nothing, therefore, can deter him from receiving Divine Revelation.

5 – Shāh 'Abdul Qādir observes: "The Prophet ﷺ was an unlettered person. The Qur'ān clarifies that Allah imparts all knowledge. He granted knowledge to the Prophet ﷺ as well." Another plausible point is that as the pen is the link between the author and his readers, Gabriel عليه السلام is the link between Allah and the Prophet ﷺ. As it is, the pen cannot excel the author or the readers. It, therefore, points to the respective excellence of the angel and the Prophet ﷺ.

6 – At the time of its birth, a baby does not have any understanding. It is Allah Who gradually imparts it knowledge and understanding, turning an ignorant person into an accomplished scholar. The same Lord transformed the unlettered Prophet ﷺ into the leader of all scholars of all times.

7 – Man originates from a clot of blood. As already pointed out, he is devoid of any understanding at the time of birth. Allah grants him knowledge. Yet he forgets all about his lowly origin. Intoxicated by wealth and worldly possessions, he takes to the path of rebellion, disregarding Allah.

8.	Verily the return is to your Lord.[8]	إِنَّ إِلَىٰ رَبِّكَ ٱلرُّجْعَىٰ ۝
9.	Did you see him who forbids?	أَرَءَيْتَ ٱلَّذِى يَنْهَىٰ ۝
10.	A servant (of Ours) when he prays?[9]	عَبْدًا إِذَا صَلَّىٰ ۝
11.	Have you considered, if he is guided?	أَرَءَيْتَ إِن كَانَ عَلَى ٱلْهُدَىٰ ۝
12.	Or if he commands piety?	أَوْ أَمَرَ بِٱلتَّقْوَىٰ ۝
13.	See, if he rejects it as false and turns away.[10]	أَرَءَيْتَ إِن كَذَّبَ وَتَوَلَّىٰ ۝
14.	Does he not realise that Allah watches him?[11]	أَلَمْ يَعْلَم بِأَنَّ ٱللَّهَ يَرَىٰ ۝

8 – Allah creates man in the first place and it is to Him that he will ultimately return. Then he will taste the fatal consequences of his unbelief and rebellion.

9 – It is the height of rebellion on man's part that he does not surrender himself to Allah. He cannot even endure the sight of other human beings submitting to their Lord. These verses allude to the accursed Abū Jahl who tormented the Prophet ﷺ whenever he observed the latter praying.

10 – Had man followed Truth and engaged in goodness, it would have turned him into Allah's perfect servant. However, if man disobeys Allah, it does not harm Him in the least (*Mūḍiḥ al-Qur'ān* and *Rūḥ al-Ma'ānī*).

11 – Allah watches both the misdeeds of the wicked and the humility and single-minded devotion of the pious.

15. Nay, if he does not give up	كَلَّا لَئِن لَّمْ يَنتَهِ
We Will seize him and drag him by his forelock.[12]	لَنَسْفَعًا بِٱلنَّاصِيَةِ ﴿١٥﴾
16. The forelock of the lying sinner.[13]	نَاصِيَةٍ كَاذِبَةٍ خَاطِئَةٍ ﴿١٦﴾
17. Now let him call members of his company.	فَلْيَدْعُ نَادِيَهُۥ ﴿١٧﴾
18. We will also call Our guards.[14]	سَنَدْعُ ٱلزَّبَانِيَةَ ﴿١٨﴾

12 – The Prophet ﷺ is told that the wicked deliberately disobey and rebel, notwithstanding their perception of the Truth. The Qur'ān warns such people that if they do not mend their ways, they will be dragged like animals while being held by their hair.

13 – Their heads are full of falsehood and sin. It appears that evil has permeated each fibre of their body.

14 – Once Abū Jahl sought to deter the Prophet ﷺ from praying. When the Prophet ﷺ tried to stop him, he retorted: "Do you not know that I command the largest number of followers in Makkah." The Qur'ān asks him to summon the members of his group to rescue him. For Allah will direct His angels to punish them. Everybody will see who will ultimately triumph. Even after a few days, it was evident on the Badr battleground that the Muslims cut Abū Jahl into pieces. As to his abiding humiliation, it will be inflicted upon him on the Day of Judgement when the angels of Hell will hurl him into Hellfire.

According to reports, once when Abū Jahl observed the Prophet ﷺ praying, he proceeded towards him in order to hurt him. However, before nearing the Prophet ﷺ, he hastily returned. On being asked why, he said that he had witnessed a trench of fire separating him from the Prophet ﷺ. Creatures with wings were

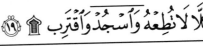

19. Nay, do not obey him.
Prostrate and draw near.[15]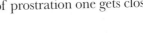

around the trench, hence he returned in haste. The Prophet ﷺ added: "Had he proceeded any further, the angels would have shred his body into innumerable pieces." What is said in verse 18 of this *Sūrah* came true regarding Abū Jahl in this life itself. Most Qur'ānic scholars take *az-zabāniyah* to be the angels of Hell.

15 – The Prophet ﷺ is directed to disregard the misdeeds of the unbelievers. He should not pay any heed to them. Rather, he should focus his attention on worshipping Allah wherever he is. By prostrating before Him, he will gain proximity to Him. It is clarified in *Ḥadīth* literature that in the posture of prostration one gets closest to Allah.

* * *

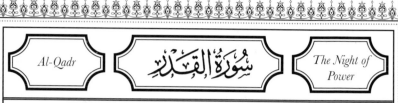

Al-Qadr سُوْرَةُ الْقَدْرِ The Night of Power

In the name of Allah, Most Compassionate, Most Merciful.

1. Indeed, We have revealed it on the Night of Power.[1] إِنَّاۤ أَنزَلْنَٰهُ فِى لَيْلَةِ ٱلْقَدْرِ ١

2. And do you know what the Night of Power is? وَمَاۤ أَدْرَىٰكَ مَا لَيْلَةُ ٱلْقَدْرِ ٢

3. The Night of Power is better than a thousand months.[2] لَيْلَةُ ٱلْقَدْرِ خَيْرٌ مِّنْ أَلْفِ شَهْرٍ ٣

4. In it the angels and the spirit descend تَنَزَّلُ ٱلْمَلَٰئِكَةُ وَٱلرُّوحُ فِيهَا

By the leave of their Lord[3] with the decree for every affair.[4] بِإِذْنِ رَبِّهِم مِّن كُلِّ أَمْرٍ ٤

1 – The Qur'ān was sent down to the world on this blessed night from the Guarded Tablet. Perhaps, it was on the same blessed night that the Messengers were deputed to the world. We have discussed at length the Qur'ānic allusion to the blessed night in our commentary on *Sūrah ad-Dukhān*. Those relevant notes should be re-studied.

2 – Doing good on that night is equivalent to doing good for one thousand months or even more.

3 – By Allah's leave, the Holy Spirit – Gabriel ﷺ – descends, surrounded by a multitude of angels in order to bless all mankind. It is also likely that the expression *ar-Rūḥ* stands for a creature other than the angels. Whatever be the case, this blessed night stands out for its special features and halo.

4 – The angels descend in order to make arrangements for the next year, as assigned to them by Allah. Almost the same points feature in *Sūrah ad-Dukhān*. Alternatively, the reference might be to all the

5. It is all peace!⁵ till the dawn.⁶	سَلَٰمٌ هِىَ حَتَّىٰ مَطۡلَعِ ٱلۡفَجۡرِ ۝

good deeds of which the tiding is given by the angel. And Allah knows best.

5 – This night is characterised by peace, tranquillity and devotion. Those devoted to Allah experience spiritual ecstasy while worshipping. This on account of the blessings brought by the angels on this particular night. According to some reports, Gabriel and all the angels engaged in worshipping and glorifying Allah send invocations and blessings for those praying. They supplicate that the devout servants of Allah be showered with Divine Mercy and blessings.

6 – This phenomenon lasts from dusk till dawn. Therefore the whole night is known as the blessed night.

The Qur'ān clarifies that this night falls in the month of *Ramaḍān* [*al-Baqarah* 2:185]. It is stated further in authentic *Ḥadīth* literature that this night should be searched for in the odd nights of the last ten nights of *Ramaḍān*. It is generally assumed that the 27th night of *Ramaḍān* is the blessed night. And Allah knows best. *'Ulamā'*, however, clarify that a particular night is not to be designated as the blessed night for every *Ramaḍān* in that this might change every year.

* * *

Al-Bayyinah   سُوْرَةُ الْبَيِّنَةِ   *The Clear Sign*

In the name of Allah, Most Compassionate, Most Merciful.	بِسْمِ اللَّهِ الرَّحْمَٰنِ الرَّحِيمِ
1. It is not (conceivable) that the unbelievers	لَمْ يَكُنِ الَّذِينَ كَفَرُوا
Among the People of the Book and the polytheists[1]	مِنْ أَهْلِ الْكِتَابِ وَالْمُشْرِكِينَ
Were giving up until the Clear Sign reached them.	مُنفَكِّينَ حَتَّىٰ تَأْتِيَهُمُ الْبَيِّنَةُ ۝
2. A Messenger from Allah	رَسُولٌ مِّنَ اللَّهِ
Reciting to them from the pure scroll.[2]	يَتْلُو صُحُفًا مُّطَهَّرَةً ۝
3. In it are eternal books.[3]	فِيهَا كُتُبٌ قَيِّمَةٌ ۝

1 – Jews and Christians constitute the People of the Book while the polytheists are the communities engaged in idolatry or fire worship. They had not been granted any Scripture.

2 – All major world faiths had been corrupted before the Prophet's advent. Everyone was proud of his error. No saint or king could make them revert to their original faith. The only way out was the advent of an outstanding Messenger aided by the Word of Allah which would first transform a whole country through its guidance. At a later date, by dint of his excellent teachings and valour he was to reform the whole world. The Prophet ﷺ, therefore, appeared reciting the Word of Allah which constitutes the Qur'ān.

3 – Each Qur'ānic *Sūrah* is a whole in itself. Alternatively, this might mean that it embodies the essence of all the Scriptures which predate the Qur'ān. The Qur'ānic expression *kutub qayyimah* may refer to

4. And the people of the Book had differed	وَمَا تَفَرَّقَ ٱلَّذِينَ أُوتُوا ٱلْكِتَٰبَ
Only after the Clear Sign reached them.[4]	إِلَّا مِنۢ بَعْدِ مَا جَآءَتْهُمُ ٱلْبَيِّنَةُ ٤
5. And they had been commanded only to worship Allah.	وَمَآ أُمِرُوٓا۟ إِلَّا لِيَعْبُدُوا۟ ٱللَّهَ
For Him is all worship exclusively (as on the way of Abraham).[5]	مُخْلِصِينَ لَهُ ٱلدِّينَ حُنَفَآءَ

branches of knowledge. Qur'ānic knowledge is characterised by soundness and balance.

4 – There is no doubt about the Prophet ﷺ or the Qur'ān. The People of the Book oppose him only out of spite. Some People of the Book reject him outright. However, the just and pious among them embraced the new faith. The People of the Book were supposed to bury their mutual differences and pledge their faith to the Messenger, whose advent they had been looking forward to for centuries. However, prompted by hostility they were divided all the more after the Prophet's appearance. This is the account of the response by the People of the Book. As to the attitude of the ignorant polytheists, the less is said, the better it will be.

Shāh 'Abdul 'Azīz took al-Bayyinah to mean the Prophet Jesus عليه السلام. As he appeared with clear Signs, the Jews turned into his worst enemies. Then the Christians were divided among themselves owing to their own selfish interests. What is said is that a Prophet's advent or the sending down of the Scripture alone does not suffice, if Allah does not guide a community to follow that Messenger and Scripture. Notwithstanding the abundance of guidance, those not inclined to the Truth incur the same loss and self-destruction.

5 – Believers should shun falsehood of all varieties and turn to worshipping the One True God. Like the faithful Abraham, they should devote themselves, heart and soul, to the One True God. They should not take any as sovereign besides Allah in matters of law and creation.

And that they maintain the Prayer and pay *Zakāh*.

وَيُقِيمُوا۟ ٱلصَّلَوٰةَ وَيُؤۡتُوا۟ ٱلزَّكَوٰةَ

And this is the sound Faith.[6]

وَذَٰلِكَ دِينُ ٱلۡقَيِّمَةِ ۝

6. The unbelievers

إِنَّ ٱلَّذِينَ كَفَرُوا۟

Among the people of the Book and the polytheists

مِنۡ أَهۡلِ ٱلۡكِتَٰبِ وَٱلۡمُشۡرِكِينَ

Will be in the Hellfire. They will abide therein.[7]

فِى نَارِ جَهَنَّمَ خَٰلِدِينَ فِيهَآ

They are the worst of creatures.[8]

أُو۟لَٰٓئِكَ هُمۡ شَرُّ ٱلۡبَرِيَّةِ ۝

7. Those who believe and do good,

إِنَّ ٱلَّذِينَ ءَامَنُوا۟ وَعَمِلُوا۟ ٱلصَّٰلِحَٰتِ

They are the best of creatures.[9]

أُو۟لَٰٓئِكَ هُمۡ خَيۡرُ ٱلۡبَرِيَّةِ ۝

---

6 – Common to all faiths are these points. The Prophet ﷺ expounds the same message. It is strange that the unbelievers resent such pure and perfect teachings.

7 – Whether it is the People of the Book or the unbelievers and notwithstanding their claim that they possess knowledge, all will meet the same fate – Hell – and they will not find a way out.

8 – They are worse than even beasts. A similar point is made in verse 44 of *Sūrah al-Furqān*.

9 – Those having firm conviction in all the Messengers and Scriptures and who are engaged in doing good stand out as the best of creatures. Some of these pious people even excel the angels.

8. Their reward is with their Lord	جَزَآؤُهُمْ عِندَ رَبِّهِمْ
Gardens of Eternity beneath which rivers flow.	جَنَّـٰتُ عَدْنٍ تَجْرِى مِن تَحْتِهَا ٱلْأَنْهَـٰرُ
They will abide therein for ever.	خَـٰلِدِينَ فِيهَآ أَبَدًا
Allah is pleased with them and they are pleased with Him.[10]	رَّضِىَ ٱللَّهُ عَنْهُمْ وَرَضُوا۟ عَنْهُ
This is for him who fears his Lord.[11]	ذَٰلِكَ لِمَنْ خَشِىَ رَبَّهُۥ ۝

10 – Apart from the Gardens and Springs of Paradise, their greatest reward is Allah's vision, which is the underlying spirit of all the bounties of Paradise.

11 – Not everyone can attain this exalted status. It is reserved only for those who fear Allah's displeasure. Accordingly, they never approach evil.

* * *

Az-Zalzalah	سُوْرَةُ الزَّلْزَلَةِ	The Earthquake

In the name of Allah, Most Compassionate, Most Merciful.	بِسْمِ اللهِ الرَّحْمٰنِ الرَّحِيْمِ
1. When the earth is shaken by its earthquake.[1]	إِذَا زُلْزِلَتِ الْأَرْضُ زِلْزَالَهَا ۝
2. And the earth throws out its burden.[2]	وَأَخْرَجَتِ الْأَرْضُ أَثْقَالَهَا ۝
3. And man will say what has happened to it.[3]	وَقَالَ الْإِنْسَانُ مَا لَهَا ۝
4. That Day the earth will disclose its affairs.	يَوْمَئِذٍ تُحَدِّثُ أَخْبَارَهَا ۝
5. This because your Lord will ask it to do so.[4]	بِأَنَّ رَبَّكَ أَوْحٰى لَهَا ۝

1 – Allah will subject the whole earth to a severe earthquake. Its impact will be so devastating that it will destroy all structures, mountains and trees. The earth will look like a level ground. It will facilitate the holding of the Grand Assembly. This will happen after the blowing of the second trumpet.

2 – The earth will release all that is inside it, as for example, dead bodies or precious metals such as gold and silver. However, there will be no one to claim it. Everyone will realise the utter uselessness of these metals which caused so much violence among human beings.

3 – After being resurrected and witnessing the effect of the earthquake, man will ask in utter amazement what happened to the earth to subject it to such a violent shaking.

4 – The earth will declare all the misdeeds committed on its surface as also all the good deeds performed. For example, it will inform that so and so offered Prayer, or committed theft or murder. In other

6. The Day people
will be in various bands[5]

يَوْمَئِذٍ يَصْدُرُ ٱلنَّاسُ

So that their record be
shown to them.[6]

أَشْتَاتًا لِّيُرَوْا۟ أَعْمَٰلَهُمْ ٦

7. So whoever does an
atom's weight of good

فَمَن يَعْمَلْ مِثْقَالَ ذَرَّةٍ خَيْرًا

Will find it.

يَرَهُۥ ٧

8. And whoever does an
atom's weight of evil

وَمَن يَعْمَلْ مِثْقَالَ ذَرَّةٍ شَرًّا

Will find it.[7]

يَرَهُۥ ٨

words, all that happens on the face of the earth is being recorded.
The same will become public knowledge by Allah's leave on the
Day of Judgement.

5 – The dead will appear as communities as they will rise from their
graves to appear for the Reckoning. There will be a community of
drunkards, another of fornicators and others of wrongdoers, thieves
and other sinners. Alternatively, the verse might mean that after
their return from the Grand Assembly, men will be placed under
different groups. Some groups will enter Paradise while others will
be consigned to Hell.

6 – Everyone will see his record of deeds on the Day of Judgement.
It will bring humiliation upon the sinners and vindicate the
superiority of the pious. This verse can, thus, be interpreted in the
sense that the consequences of good and bad deeds will become
manifest on that Day.

7 – Each and every deed committed by everyone will be displayed
before them. Likewise, everyone will watch how Allah recompenses
each and everyone.

***

Al-'Ādiyāt — سُوْرَةُ الْعَادِيَاتِ — The Coursers

In the name of Allah, Most Compassionate, Most Merciful.

1. By the coursers that pant.

وَٱلْعَٰدِيَٰتِ ضَبْحًا ﴿١﴾

2. And the sparks of fire by their hooves.[1]

فَٱلْمُورِيَٰتِ قَدْحًا ﴿٢﴾

3. And raiding at dawn.[2]

فَٱلْمُغِيرَٰتِ صُبْحًا ﴿٣﴾

4. They raise dust therein.[3]

فَأَثَرْنَ بِهِۦ نَقْعًا ﴿٤﴾

5. Then they enter the midst of the army.[4]

فَوَسَطْنَ بِهِۦ جَمْعًا ﴿٥﴾

1 – Reference is made to the sparks of fire produced by the hooves of galloping horses.

2 – It was customary in the Arabia of that time to raid the enemy in the dark hours of the night so that the enemy could not see their movements as they approached. This was regarded as an act of bravery.

3 – Reference is made to the swift movement of galloping horses at dawn while the whole atmosphere is characterised by an intense cold and humidity caused by the dew. The movement of these horses raised much dust.

4 – They swoop on the enemy in a fearless manner. It is likely that the oath is by the horse in a literal sense, or this may signify the believers' cavalry. Shāh 'Abdul Qādir states: "This oath is in the name of those waging *Jihād*. No deed is better or greater than participating in *Jihād* and pledging one's willingness to lay down one's life in Allah's cause."

6.	Verily man is ungrateful to his Lord.[5]	إِنَّ ٱلْإِنسَٰنَ لِرَبِّهِۦ لَكَنُودٌ ٦
7.	And verily man is a witness to it.[6]	وَإِنَّهُۥ عَلَىٰ ذَٰلِكَ لَشَهِيدٌ ٧

5 – The commitment and spirit of self-sacrifice of those waging *Jihād* indicates their gratitude and devotion to Allah. Those who fail to utilise the faculties granted them by Allah, in the way prescribed by Him, betray their ingratitude and foolishness. On a little reflection, even the conduct of the horse bears out that such men are contemptible who do not spend their resources in the prescribed way. For they are the ones sustained by the Lord, draw upon His numerous favours yet fail to obey Him. Such are worse than animals. The master provides the horse with a little fodder. For this small favour the horse stakes its life in the service of its master. It unquestioningly follows his directives, gallops and exerts itself at the command of its master. The same valour is displayed by the horse on the battlefield. It does not shy away from arrows and bullets in the cause of its master. At times, it sacrifices its life in order to defend and support him. Does man not learn any lesson from the conduct of the horse that he too should serve his Master in the same faithful manner? Indeed, man is ungrateful and undeserving of any good treatment. For he is not loyal to his Master in the degree displayed by the horse and dog.

6 – Man is a witness to the sacrifices of those waging *Jihād* and the excellent conduct of their horses. Yet still he does not take any heed.

Our commentary reflects the spirit of the translation of this verse. Most Qur'ānic scholars, however, interpret the verse in the sense that man himself bears testimony to his ingratitude. If man were to listen to the voice of his conscience, he would realise his ingratitude. Some classical authorities take the verse to mean that Allah watches man's ingratitude.

8. And man is passionate in his love of wealth.[7]

وَإِنَّهُ لِحُبِّ ٱلۡخَيۡرِ لَشَدِيدٌ ۝

9. Does he not know

۞ أَفَلَا يَعۡلَمُ

That whoever is in the grave will be resurrected?

إِذَا بُعۡثِرَ مَا فِي ٱلۡقُبُورِ ۝

10. And whatever is within the breast will be brought to light?[8]

وَحُصِّلَ مَا فِي ٱلصُّدُورِ ۝

11. Verily their Lord will be All-aware of them that Day.[9]

إِنَّ رَبَّهُم بِهِمۡ يَوۡمَئِذٍ لَّخَبِيرٌ ۝

7 – Man is blinded by his greed, lust, miserliness and pleasure-seeking. Engrossed in worldliness he abandons his True Benefactor, and fails to realise what punishment is in store for his misconduct.

8 – Soon there will come a time when the dead will rise from their graves. All that is concealed deep inside each heart will become public knowledge. At this point, the unbelievers will recognise that their wealth cannot avail them. Ungrateful men will not find a way to escape. Had they realised this Truth, they would not have devoted themselves to the worship of wealth and not committed such misdeeds.

9 – Allah's knowledge embraces both the outward and inward affairs of everyone. His knowledge comes to everyone's notice on the Day of Judgement. It is not possible for anyone to deny His Omniscience.

* * *

Al-Qāri'ah — سُورَةُ الْقَارِعَةِ — The Striking Hour

In the name of Allah, Most Compassionate, Most Merciful.

بِسْمِ اللَّهِ الرَّحْمَٰنِ الرَّحِيمِ

1. The Clatterer!

الْقَارِعَةُ ۝

2. What is it that Clatters?

مَا الْقَارِعَةُ ۝

3. And do you know what the Clatterer is?[1]

وَمَا أَدْرَاكَ مَا الْقَارِعَةُ ۝

4. The Day mankind will be

Like moths scattered.[2]

يَوْمَ يَكُونُ النَّاسُ كَالْفَرَاشِ الْمَبْثُوثِ ۝

5. And the mountains will be

Like carded wool.[3]

وَتَكُونُ الْجِبَالُ كَالْعِهْنِ الْمَنفُوشِ ۝

1 – The reference here is to the Day of Judgement. It will shake everyone both outwardly and inwardly. Deep inside everyone will be full of panic while there will be a deafening noise all around. It is hard to relate in words the agony which will befall man on the Last Day. Some of its details are recounted in this *Sūrah* to give an idea of the hardships to be suffered by man on that Day.

2 – Everyone will throng like moths. The simile underscores man's weakness, passionate nature and unruliness.

3 – Like carded wool, the mountains will disintegrate. This pointed reference to wool is made in order to bring out its weakness and

6.	So for him whose balance is heavy.	فَأَمَّا مَن ثَقُلَتْ مَوَازِينُهُ ۝
7.	He will be in comfort, well pleased.[4]	فَهُوَ فِي عِيشَةٍ رَّاضِيَةٍ ۝
8.	And for him whose balance is light.	وَأَمَّا مَنْ خَفَّتْ مَوَازِينُهُ ۝
9.	He will be in the pit.	فَأُمُّهُ هَاوِيَةٌ ۝
10.	And what do you know what it is?	وَمَا أَدْرَاكَ مَا هِيَهْ ۝
11.	It is the Blazing Fire.[5]	نَارٌ حَامِيَةٌ ۝

lightness. The colours of the mountains are indicated in verse 21 of *Sūrah Fāṭir*.

4 – Whoever has a good record of deeds will enjoy all comforts and pleasure. One's record will be weighty in terms of Faith, sincerity and good deeds. If one does something and it is devoid of the spirit of Faith, it will not carry any weight with Allah, a point also stated in verse 105 of *Sūrah al-Kahf*.

5 – The intense punishment to be inflicted in this part of Hell is difficult even to imagine. In a manner of speaking, it will be a blazing Hellfire. By comparison, all fire is not hot at all. May Allah protect us against it and against all modes of punishment out of His Grace and Mercy. *Āmeen*.

* * *

| At-Takāthur | سُوْرَةُ التَّكَاثُرِ | Rivalry in Worldly Increase |

In the name of Allah, Most Compassionate, Most Merciful.	
1. Greed of wealth has made you negligent.	أَلْهَىٰكُمُ التَّكَاثُرُ ۝
2. Until you visit your graves.[1]	حَتَّىٰ زُرْتُمُ الْمَقَابِرَ ۝
3. Nay, you will soon realise.	كَلَّا سَوْفَ تَعْلَمُوْنَ ۝
4. Then Nay, you will soon realise.[2]	ثُمَّ كَلَّا سَوْفَ تَعْلَمُوْنَ ۝

1 – Love of wealth, children and other worldly objects blinds man in this life. He is so much engrossed in these that he does not remember his Lord. Nor does he think about the Hereafter. All his energy is focused on amassing more and more wealth. Likewise, man is constantly engaged in a mad pursuit of power. As a result he grows totally negligent. When one dies, one realises that one has wasted one's whole life in vain pursuits. Worldly life was but a brief glitter. All worldly things will turn out to be valueless as one approaches one's end.

According to some reports, which are not very authentic, two tribes were boasting of their respective strength. While heads were counted, a group said that the graves of their dead members should also be counted. Upon adding their number, that tribe claimed a greater membership for itself. They also sought to bring to light how outstanding the deceased members of their group were. As a warning to them for such negligence and ignorance these verses were sent down. Both interpretations are, thus, equally sound.

2 – It is repeatedly stated in the Qur'ān that abundance of wealth and children will not avail anyone at all. Man will soon recognise

5. Nay, if you knew, you will gain the conviction.[3]   كَلَّا لَوْ تَعْلَمُونَ عِلْمَ ٱلْيَقِينِ ۝

6. Verily you have to see the Blazing Fire.   لَتَرَوُنَّ ٱلْجَحِيمَ ۝

7. Then you have to see it with sure vision.[4]   ثُمَّ لَتَرَوُنَّهَا عَيْنَ ٱلْيَقِينِ ۝

8. Then you will be interrogated   ثُمَّ لَتُسْـَٔلُنَّ

That Day about the delights (of the world).[5]   يَوْمَئِذٍ عَنِ ٱلنَّعِيمِ ۝

that these do not carry any weight and that one should not take pride in them. The Hereafter is too important and serious to be taken lightly. For man will soon realise that abiding pleasures can only be had in the Next Life. By comparison, the present worldly life is no more than a dream. Some fortunate people recognise this Truth in their present life. However, this Truth will dawn on everyone when they are inside the graves and on the Day of Judgement.

3 – It is a fallacious notion entertained by man that the Hereafter is unreal. Had man realised this Truth, he would have dismissed all worldly possessions, knowing that these are worthless.

4 – If man is negligent, he will end up in Hell. One cannot avoid the terrible consequences of one's misconduct. He will taste the punishment partly in *Barzakh* and will gain conviction about the same, as he will witness it in its fullness in the Hereafter.

5 – The unbelievers will be asked about the worth of their worldly joys and comforts. Or they will be interrogated about how far they discharged their obligation in return for material and spiritual favours. What steps did they take to win the pleasure of their True Benefactor and Master?

***

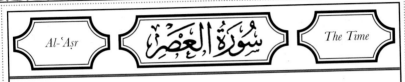

Al-'Aṣr — سُوْرَةُ الْعَصْرِ — The Time

| In the name of Allah, Most Compassionate, Most Merciful. |  |

1. By the time.[1]

إِنَّ الْإِنسَٰنَ لَفِى خُسْرٍ ٢

2. Verily man is in loss.[2]

وَٱلْعَصْرِ ١

1 – 'Aṣr literally means period or age. The oath taken refers to this. It also includes man's own age which should be regarded as a precious blessing for attaining virtue and perfection. Alternatively, the oath may be taken as with reference to the time of 'Aṣr Prayer which also happens to be the prime time of business activity. From the point of view of the *Sharī'ah* it is a blessed hour. The Prophet ﷺ is on record as saying: "Whoever misses 'Aṣr Prayer suffers a serious loss." Or the oath is a pointed reference to the Prophet's age which stands out above other periods for his advent and for the institution of the Rightly-Guided Caliphs in that both of these blessed the age in a special manner.

2 – There cannot be a greater loss than the loss of one's capital money. By the same token, man's most gracious asset, time, is gradually slipping away. If one does not accomplish anything worthwhile, one will suffer grievously. In an otherwise case, one will reap eternal rewards. On studying history and on reflecting on one's own career, it emerges that those who do not act with vision, who disregard their future and waste their time in trivial pursuits meet with loss and destruction. Man should, therefore, value time and not waste this precious asset in vain pursuits; those hours which are known as being blessed should especially be used well. While the Prophet ﷺ is alive, those present should make the most of this golden opportunity. If one is lost in negligence and error, then this

3. Except those who believe and do good	إِلَّا ٱلَّذِينَ ءَامَنُواْ وَعَمِلُواْ ٱلصَّـٰلِحَـٰتِ
And exhort one another to the Truth	وَتَوَاصَوْاْ بِٱلْحَقِّ
And exhort one another to perseverance.[3]	وَتَوَاصَوْاْ بِٱلصَّبْرِ ۝

constitutes one's greatest loss. Blessed are the souls who strive to earn good in this life and actively pursue the way of Truth. They are the ones more specifically mentioned in verse 3 of this *Sūrah*.

3 – In order to avoid loss man must bear in mind the following four points:

i) he should first profess faith in Allah and His Messenger and have firm conviction in their teachings and promises relating to both worlds;

ii) this conviction should not be merely verbal or confined to the heart and mind. It should be reflected in one's deeds. One's conduct should be indicative of firm faith;

iii) one should not rest content with improving one's conduct. Rather, one should work for the welfare and prosperity of the whole community. Whenever two Muslims meet, they should exhort each other to practise true faith and pursue the way of Truth in every human activity;

iv) Muslims should exhort one another that they bear with perseverance the hardships suffered in the cause of Truth and the reform of the community. Nothing should shake one's commitment.

Those possessing all four characteristics are perfect souls. They will help others gain perfection and they will enjoy an eternal existence. Their good deeds will always serve as a role model. It will increase their reward. This short *Sūrah* encompasses the essentials and spirit of Faith. Imām Shāfiʿī aptly remarked: "Had only this single Qurʾānic *Sūrah* been sent down, it would have sufficed for the guidance of those endowed with understanding." In the early days of Islam when two Muslims met each other they would recite this *Sūrah* before they parted company.

Al-Humazah	سُوْرَةُ الْهُمَزَةِ	*The Slanderer*

In the name of Allah, Most Compassionate, Most Merciful.

1. Woe for every slandering and fault-finding one.[1]

وَيْلٌ لِّكُلِّ هُمَزَةٍ لُّمَزَةٍ ۝

2. Who hoards wealth and counts it.[2]

ٱلَّذِى جَمَعَ مَالًا وَعَدَّدَهُۥ ۝

3. He thinks that his wealth will be there for him for ever.[3]

يَحْسَبُ أَنَّ مَالَهُۥٓ أَخْلَدَهُۥ ۝

4. Nay, he will be thrown into the crushing one.[4]

كَلَّا لَيُنۢبَذَنَّ فِى ٱلْحُطَمَةِ ۝

---

1 – Such a person is disregardful of his failings whereas he reproaches others, looking down upon them. He is always engaged in finding fault with others.

2 – The main reason behind reproaching is man's arrogance, which in turn is caused by his love of wealth. He abuses all his talents, energy and resources in amassing wealth and he does not spend a single penny out of miserliness. He keeps a very strict account of his income lest he might spend anything on charity. It is a common sight to note the miserly rich counting and recounting their wealth. It delights them greatly.

3 – It appears from his conduct as if his wealth will be there with him forever. He mistakenly believes that his wealth will defend him against all calamities, both earthly and heavenly.

4 – This notion is absolutely false. One cannot carry wealth even to the grave. It is out of the question that one will be rescued by wealth on the Day of Judgement. One has to leave behind all possessions upon death. Yet miserly ones will be hurled into Hell.

5. And what do you think the crushing one is?	وَمَآ أَدْرَىٰكَ مَا ٱلْحُطَمَةُ ۝
6. It is Allah's Fire which is kindled.	نَارُ ٱللَّهِ ٱلْمُوقَدَةُ ۝
7. It rises up to the hearts.[5]	ٱلَّتِى تَطَّلِعُ عَلَى ٱلْأَفْئِدَةِ ۝
8. It shall overtake them.[6]	إِنَّهَا عَلَيْهِم مُّؤْصَدَةٌ ۝
9. In tall pillars.[7]	فِى عَمَدٍ مُّمَدَّدَةٍ ۝

5 – Let it be clarified that this is not some fire ignited by man. Rather, it is heavenly fire from Allah. It is impossible to appreciate its real nature. It discriminates between the pious and the wicked and takes note of everyone's intentions. Whoever is devoid of faith is burnt to ashes by it whereas it spares those blessed with faith. Its heat afflicts both the body and the heart. Rather, it proceeds from the heart to envelop the body finally. Though both the body and the soul of the wicked will roast in fire, still they will not die. The inmates of Hell will fervently wish that death will put an end to their existence. However, their wish will not be fulfilled. May Allah protect us from this and all other forms of punishment out of His Mercy and Grace. *Āmeen.*

6 – Once the unbelievers are inside Hell, its gates will be sealed. They will have no way out. They will roast in Hellfire forever.

7 – The flames will be as high as the columns of a building or the inmates of Hell will be tied to high pillars so that they do not move even an inch while they are punished. Any movement could slightly relieve them of their punishment. Some scholars hold that the entry point of Hell will be sealed with high columns. And Allah knows best.

* * *

Al-Fīl	سُوْرَةُ الْفِيْلِ	*The Elephant*

In the name of Allah, Most Compassionate, Most Merciful.

بِسْمِ اللهِ الرَّحْمٰنِ الرَّحِيْمِ

1. Did you not see how Allah dealt with

The People of the Elephant.[1]

أَلَمْ تَرَ كَيْفَ فَعَلَ رَبُّكَ بِأَصْحٰبِ الْفِيْلِ ۝

2. Did He not turn the tables upon them?[2]

أَلَمْ يَجْعَلْ كَيْدَهُمْ فِيْ تَضْلِيْلٍ ۝

3. And sent down against them birds in flocks.

وَأَرْسَلَ عَلَيْهِمْ طَيْرًا أَبَابِيْلَ ۝

4. Who pelted upon them clay stones.[3]

تَرْمِيْهِمْ بِحِجَارَةٍ مِّنْ سِجِّيْلٍ ۝

1 – The Makkan unbelievers are asked about the treatment meted out by Allah to the People of the Elephant. This event happened before the Prophet's birth. It was a well-known event familiar to everyone in Arabia. Since it was fairly recent, they are asked whether they had witnessed it.

2 – The invaders intended to demolish the Ka'bah in order to divert the pilgrims to the structure erected by them. They did not, however, succeed in their nefarious design. Allah frustrated all their plans. While they planned to demolish the Ka'bah, they themselves were destroyed.

3 – Here is an outline of the story of the People of the Elephant. Abrahah was the ruler of Yemen, who had been delegated power by the Abyssinian king. As he observed the pilgrims visiting the Ka'bah in large numbers, he thought of diverting them to his town. He therefore planned to raise a Church in his town, to be adorned with the best material. It would make people abandon the Ka'bah, which

5. And He reduced them to devoured chaff.[4]	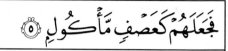

was known for its simplicity and draw people to his highly ornate Church instead. It would bring to an end the pilgrimage to Makkah. Accordingly, he built the Church in Sana, a major town in Yemen. He lavishly spent money on the building and decorating of this Church. Yet it did not attract any pilgrims. The Arabs were outraged when they learnt of his plan, especially the Quraysh. One of them visited the Church and defecated there. It is reported that some Arabs set it on fire, severely damaging it. By way of revenge, Abrahah decided to invade the Ka'bah. He proceeded with a huge army and many elephants. He destroyed all the tribes *en route*, who sought to arrest his march. 'Abd al-Muttalib, the Prophet's grandfather, was the leader of the Quraysh and Custodian of the Ka'bah. On coming to know about Abrahah's march, he directed people to ensure their own defence. For Allah would defend the Ka'bah in that it happens to be His house. As Abrahah did not face any resistance, he was confident of his demolition plan succeeding. For there was no one to oppose him. As he reached a valley near Makkah, there appeared flocks of birds, carrying small stones in their beaks and claws. These birds rained these stones down on Abrahah's army. As a miracle, these stones proved more fatal than bullets or any other weapon. As these hit a man, he collapsed to the ground, his body badly disfigured. Many perished on the spot. Even those who managed to escape later suffered a very painful death. This incident happened only 50 days before the Prophet's birth. It was, in a sense, a heavenly Sign of his advent. Some even hold that this incident happened on the Day the Prophet ﷺ was born. Implicit in it was the message that as Allah has defended His house in an extraordinary way, He would also protect His Messenger, the future custodian of the Ka'bah. It would not be possible for Christians or the adherents of any other faith to oppress sincere devotees of the Ka'bah. Nor would any be able to harm the Ka'bah.

4 – That is, the chaff – the husks left over when the grain is devoured by cattle. They were reduced to pieces, appearing as useless as stubble.

Quraysh	سُورَةُ قُرَيْشٍ	Quraysh

In the name of Allah, Most Compassionate, Most Merciful.

بِسْمِ اللَّهِ الرَّحْمَٰنِ الرَّحِيمِ

1. For the familiarity of the Quraysh.

لِإِيلَٰفِ قُرَيْشٍ ١

2. Their familiarity (facilitate for them)

إِۦلَٰفِهِمْ

With the journeys in winter and summer.[1]

رِحْلَةَ ٱلشِّتَآءِ وَٱلصَّيْفِ ٢

3. Let them worship the Lord of this House.

فَلْيَعْبُدُوا۟ رَبَّ هَٰذَا ٱلْبَيْتِ ٣

4. He Who fed them in hunger

ٱلَّذِىٓ أَطْعَمَهُم مِّن جُوعٍ

And blessed them with peace against fear.[2]

وَءَامَنَهُم مِّنْ خَوْفٍۭ ٤

1 – Their prestige as custodians of the Ka'bah enabled, by Allah's Grace and Protection, the Quraysh caravans to journey without any fear of danger.

2 – No corn was grown in Makkah. Therefore, the Makkans undertook two business journeys every year in winter and summer. In winter they travelled to Yemen and in summer to Syria, which was a fertile, prosperous country. Being the custodians of the Ka'bah, they were treated well by everyone. People would serve them and not pose any threat to their life and property. They earned a good profit in their business deals. In times of peace they subsisted on their earnings. Around Makkah there was much lawlessness. However, the Quraysh were safe against any attack in view of their association with the Ka'bah. This Divine favour upon them is reiterated in these verses. The Quraysh are told that they

earn their livelihood, thanks to their link with the Ka'bah. On account of this, they enjoy peace and security. Allah defended them against the People of the Elephant. Given this, it is strange that they do not worship Him. Likewise, they are asked why they persecute His Messenger. This amounts to the utmost ingratitude on their part.

* * *

| Al-Māʿūn | سُورَةُ الْمَاعُونِ | The Small Kindnesses |

| In the name of Allah, Most Compassionate, Most Merciful. |  |

| 1. Did you see him who | |
| Rejects the Day of Judgement as false?[1] | يُكَذِّبُ بِالدِّينِ ۝ |

| 2. He is the one who pushes away the orphan.[2] | فَذَٰلِكَ الَّذِي يَدُعُّ الْيَتِيمَ ۝ |

| 3. And he does not exhort the feeding of the poor.[3] | وَلَا يَحُضُّ عَلَىٰ طَعَامِ الْمِسْكِينِ ۝ |

| 4. Woe for such who pray. | فَوَيْلٌ لِّلْمُصَلِّينَ ۝ |

1 – That is those who think that justice will not be enforced, who think that they will not be recompensed for their good and evil deeds. Some scholars interpret the expression *ad-dīn* as the religious community. Taken in this sense, the reference is to those who reject religion as false. For such faith is totally unimportant.

2 – Far from showing any compassion or sympathy towards the poor and needy, they mistreat them.

3 – They do not look after the poor. Nor do they exhort others to do the same. It goes without saying that looking after the orphan and the needy and showing sympathy to them is an article of faith in every religion. These are universal virtues recognised by every sane person. However, those who are devoid of even such fundamental moral principles cannot be taken as human beings. They do not have any concern for faith and for Allah.

5.	Those who are heedless of their Prayers.[4]	اَلَّذِيْنَ هُمْ عَنْ صَلَاتِهِمْ سَاهُوْنَ ۝
6.	Those who make of it a show.[5]	اَلَّذِيْنَ هُمْ يُرَآءُوْنَ ۝
7.	And those who refuse small favours (to others).[6]	وَيَمْنَعُوْنَ الْمَاعُوْنَ ۝

4 – They are absolutely ignorant of the Prayer and its underlying objective. Nor do they recognise its significance. It is all the same for them whether they offer the Prayer or not, or pray at the appointed hour or not. While lost in worldly activities, they fail to perform the Prayer at its appointed hour. Even when they do pray, they do so without any devotion or concentration. It does not occur to them that during the Prayer they stand face to face with the Best and Most Powerful of all Judges. Allah is not interested only in the observance of the rituals of the Prayer. Rather, He reckons our intention. What is noted is whether one possesses faith and humility. All these points are implicit in verse 5 of this *Sūrah*. This point is explained by many classical authorities.

5 – Not only in Prayer, but all the deeds of the hypocrites betray their opportunism and pretence. While disregarding their Creator, they seek only to please and impress their fellow men.

6 – Not only do they refuse to pay *Zakāh* and alms, they are not even prepared to help others by lending them objects of daily use such as water containers, rope, cooking pots, a thread and needle, etc. It is customary to give these things on loan. However, they are so much carried away by their own miserliness and wickedness that they do not even observe basic courtesy. In the face of their blatant hypocrisy, their Prayers will not avail them. If one claims to be a Muslim who prays and still does not act sincerely towards Allah and fellow human beings, then one's faith is pointless and one's Prayer soulless. Such hypocrisy is exhibited by those accursed persons who do not have any belief in Allah and in the true faith.

| Al-Kauthar | سُوْرَةُ الْكَوْثَرِ | The Abundance |

In the name of Allah, Most Compassionate, Most Merciful.

1. Verily We have granted you *al-Kauthar*.[1]

2. So pray for your Lord and sacrifice.[2]

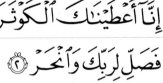

---

1 – Literally *al-Kauthar* means abundant good. As for its interpretation, as many as 26 views are recorded in *al-Baḥr al-Muḥīṭ*. According to its author, the most plausible rendering is the bounty in abundance, which relates to both the worlds and which was conferred upon the Prophet ﷺ and his community. Of the numerous such bounties, one is the *Kauthar* Fountain. The Prophet ﷺ will offer its drink to his *ummah* on the Day of Judgement. O the Most Merciful of the Merciful! Include me among those who would draw upon it on the Last Day. *Āmeen*.

That there will be a fountain bearing the name of *al-Kauthar* is mentioned in numerous and consistent *aḥādīth* according to some *Ḥadīth* scholars it has reached the stage of *tawātur*. Therefore it requires every Muslim to believe in it. Its special properties have been spelled out in *Ḥadīth* literature. It is also confirmed that its water will be available on the Day of Judgement, though it is situated in Paradise. Most scholars reconcile the two statements thus that the Spring is in Paradise while its water will be pooled in a fountain in the Grand Assembly. Both of them are known as *al-Kauthar*. And Allah Alone knows the Truth.

2 – The expression of gratitude for such a bounteous favour should be tremendous. The Prophet ﷺ should devote himself heart and soul to worshipping and serving his Lord. Of all modes of worship, Prayer is the most outstanding. Likewise, among monetary modes of

3. Verily it is your enemy who will be childless.[3]

worship, sacrificing animals stands out above others. For it signifies one's willingness to sacrifice one's own life. Animal sacrifice was instituted in order to replace self-sacrifice. This point comes out sharply in the story of the Prophet Abraham ﷺ. In verse 162 of *Sūrah al-Anʿām*, the Prayer is bracketed together with animal sacrifice.

According to some reports, the expression *wanḥar* stands for placing one's hands on one's chest (in prayer). Ibn Kathīr, however rejects this interpretation and prefers the view that the expression denotes animal sacrifice. This expression indicts the polytheists in that their Prayer and sacrifice were devoted to their idols. Muslims are supposed to dedicate these to the One True God.

3 – Some unbelievers taunted the Prophet ﷺ about him not having a son. As a result, they said, he would be cast into oblivion. Such a person is known in Arabic idiom as *abtar*. This also stands for a tail-less animal. Common to both expressions is the idea that someone is without progeny. The Qurʾān asserts that one who has been granted good in abundance and whose name has been immortalised cannot be dismissed as *abtar*. Those hurling this charge are themselves utter fools. For their hostility to the Prophet ﷺ, they themselves are disgraced and traceless. The unbelievers will not leave behind any goodness. Nor will they serve as a model for posterity. In the last fourteen hundred years there have literally been hundreds of millions of Muslims who have taken pride in being the Prophet's progeny. They are spread in almost all parts of the world. His faith and his role model have been the exemplar for centuries for millions of people to emulate. The Prophet ﷺ is held in great esteem by hundreds of millions of people throughout the world. Even his worst enemies acknowledge his major contribution to social reform.

As for the Prophet's exalted status in the Hereafter, he will be publicly acclaimed. Everyone will bear out his greatness. Such a blessed personality cannot be dismissed as *abtar* by any stretch of the imagination. It is his detractors, who levelled this charge, who were lost in oblivion. No one speaks of them highly. The same fate befell those who opposed the Prophet ﷺ at various stages of human history and who acted outrageously towards him.

* * *

Al-Kāfirūn | سُورَةُ الْكَافِرُونَ | The Disbelievers

In the name of Allah, Most Compassionate, Most Merciful.

1. Say: O unbelievers![1]

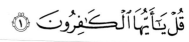

2. I do not worship what you worship.

1 – Some Quraysh chiefs offered the Prophet ﷺ the following agreement: "O Muḥammad! Let us conclude a peace treaty. You should serve our lords for a year. The next year we will worship your Lord. So doing, both parties would practise their faith." The Prophet ﷺ responded: "I seek Allah's refuge against ascribing any partner to Him even for a single moment." Then the Quraysh asked him not to condemn their lords. In return they would bear out his Messengership and worship Allah. It was against this background that the present *Sūrah* was sent down. The Prophet ﷺ recited it to them in a public meeting. In sum, this *Sūrah* proclaims a total dissociation with the ways of the polytheists and severing all ties with them. Since the Messengers are primarily concerned with obliterating polytheism, they cannot enter into such an alliance with polytheists. That Allah is the Lord is not contested by anyone. Even the Makkan polytheists conceded that they worship idols in the belief that it would bring them closer to Allah (*Sūrah az-Zumar*: 3). The main difference lay in idolatry. The offer of peace presented by the Quraysh maintained the same position that they would continue committing idolatry whereas the Prophet ﷺ should give up his belief in monotheism. This *Sūrah* rejects such an offer of peace.

3.	And you will not worship what I worship.[2]	وَلَآ أَنتُمۡ عَٰبِدُونَ مَآ أَعۡبُدُ ٣
4.	And I am not going to worship what you worshiped.	وَلَآ أَنَا۠ عَابِدٞ مَّا عَبَدتُّمۡ ٤
5.	And you will not worship what I worship.[3]	وَلَآ أَنتُمۡ عَٰبِدُونَ مَآ أَعۡبُدُ ٥

2 – The Prophet does not worship the false gods invented by the unbelievers. Nor do they worship Allah Who is Alone and Unique. They ascribe partners to Him whom the Prophet worships.

3 – The Prophet declares that he will never worship their gods. Nor will they ever devote themselves to the One True God. He being a monotheist cannot indulge in polytheism. By the same token, they being polytheists cannot be taken as monotheists. Since this statement is related to the future, it does not repeat the point made in verse 2 of this *Sūrah*.

According to some *'ulamā'*, this point is repeated in order to reinforce the contention. However, some scholars interpret it in terms of present and future happenings, as is maintained by Zamakhsharī, the great linguist and *mufassir*. Some other scholars offer the following interpretation: There is nothing common between the Prophet and the polytheists regarding the Lord or the mode of worship. The Prophet does not worship those whom they do. Rather, he worships the Lord Who does not have any partner in His Being or Attributes. Their gods do not qualify for such Lordship. Likewise, the Prophet does not worship in the manner that they do, as for example, walking round the Ka'bah in a naked state, or whistling and clapping, instead of remembering Allah. He will never worship in such a manner. They cannot worship in the manner that he does. Therefore, their ways are absolutely different.

In our opinion, these verses speak of present and future happenings. The point brought home is that the Prophet does not and would not worship their lords. Ibn Taymiyyah clarifies the

6. For you is your way
   and for me mine.[4]

لَكُمْ دِينُكُمْ وَلِيَ دِينِ ۝٦

point further in stating that the Prophet ﷺ, being the Messenger of
Allah, is not supposed to commit polytheism in any degree. Even
in the past and prior to the sending down of Revelation when all
the Makkans were engrossed in worshipping idols and trees, the
Prophet ﷺ never committed idolatry. As he had been blessed with
Divine Light and Revelation, it was out of the question that he
would ever follow them in polytheistic practices. This explains why
verse 4 of this *Sūrah* is in the past tense.

As to the conduct of the unbelievers, it is all the same both in
the past and for the future. Since they are not inclined to Truth and
are too wicked, they are never likely to worship the One True God.
Even when offering peace, they are keen on maintaining their
polytheism. As for the past and present tenses used for their
polytheism in the two verses, this implies that their gods constantly
change. As they come across anything striking or an impressive
stone, they elevate it to godhead while abandoning their earlier
idols. They had gods for each assignment and for every season, as
for example, for journeys, for sustenance, for granting children. Ibn
Qayyim has dealt extensively with the insights embodied in this
Sūrah in his *Badāeyey' al-Fawā'id*. Those interested in a deeper study
of the Qur'ān should make a point of consulting this work.

4 – Shāh 'Abdul Qādir observes: "Given the polytheists' rigid
stance, the Prophet's admonition would not avail them. Allah Alone
will settle the matter. The Prophet ﷺ is quit of the polytheists and
looks forward to Divine Judgement regarding them. He is perfectly
satisfied with the faith granted to him by Allah. Let them rejoice in
the path which they have chosen out of their wickedness. Every
party will be recompensed for its conduct."

* * *

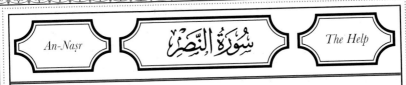

An-Naṣr سُورَةُ النَّصْرِ The Help

In the name of Allah, Most Compassionate, Most Merciful.	بِسْمِ اللَّهِ الرَّحْمَٰنِ الرَّحِيمِ
1. When Allah's help and victory arrives.[1]	 إِذَا جَاءَ نَصْرُ اللَّهِ وَالْفَتْحُ ۝
2. And you see mankind	وَرَأَيْتَ النَّاسَ
Entering the fold of Allah's faith in multitudes.[2]	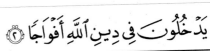 يَدْخُلُونَ فِي دِينِ اللَّهِ أَفْوَاجًا ۝

1 – The conquest of Makkah was crucial to the history of Islam. It was a decisive factor. Accordingly, all the Arab tribes had been waiting for this to happen. Prior to its conquest, people accepted Islam in small numbers. After the conquest, however, they entered the fold of Islam in throngs. Gradually, the whole Arabian Peninsula was won over to Islam. This accomplished the purpose of the Prophet's advent.

2 – The Prophet ﷺ is told that the purpose of his advent and his career has been accomplished in that faith has been perfected and the grand *khilāfah* is in place. The Prophet ﷺ should be ready for his last journey. Having finished his mission, he should devote himself completely to his final journey. He should engage more in praising and glorifying Allah and thank Him profusely for the victories and favours granted him.

3.	Celebrate the praise of your Lord	فَسَبِّحْ بِحَمْدِ رَبِّكَ
	And seek forgiveness from Him.	وَاسْتَغْفِرْهُ
	Verily He is Oft-Returning.[3]	إِنَّهُ كَانَ تَوَّابًا ٣

3 – The Prophet ﷺ is asked to seek forgiveness both for himself and for his community. That the Prophet ﷺ constantly asked for his forgiveness is stated elsewhere in this work. Our earlier notes on this subject should also be consulted. Shāh 'Abdul Qādir holds: "The Qur'ān often speaks of the promise of recompense. The unbelievers asked that it be expedited. In the last years of the Prophet's career, Makkah had been conquered and the Arab tribes had accepted Islam *en masse*. Allah's promise had come true. Therefore, the Prophet ﷺ is directed to seek forgiveness for his community so that he may fulfil the role of intercessor. This *Sūrah* was revealed towards the end of his career. He, therefore, realised that his mission in this life was over and that he was about to proceed on his last journey."

* * *

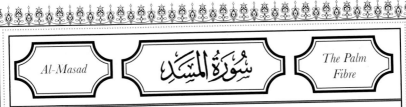

| Al-Masad | سُورَةُ المَسَدِ | The Palm Fibre |

In the name of Allah, Most Compassionate, Most Merciful.

1. The hands of Abū Lahab have perished and he has perished.[1]

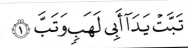

1 – Abū Lahab was the Prophet's real uncle. His name was ʿAbd al-ʿUzzā ibn ʿAbd al-Muṭṭalib. However, motivated by unbelief and callousness he was one of the Prophet's arch enemies. Whenever the Prophet ﷺ addressed a public meeting, he used to hurl stones at him. This hurt the Prophet ﷺ and he bled profusely. Apart from obstructing the Prophet ﷺ in the above manner, he also used to proclaim: "O people! Do not listen to him. He is a liar and a man of no faith. He promises bounties after death, though these are not visible at all. Had this been true, we would have seen these bounties with our eyes. Let your hands perish in that I do not perceive any truth in what Muḥammad says." Once the Prophet ﷺ called out at everyone while standing at the Ṣafā hillock. Everyone responded to his call and assembled there. The Prophet ﷺ invited them in a highly effective manner to embrace Islam. Abū Lahab was also present there. According to some reports, he made a gesture with his hands and said: "May you perish! Have you assembled us only for this?" It is cited in *Rūḥ al-Maʿānī* that he picked up a stone and was about to throw it at the Prophet ﷺ. As his opposition to the Prophet ﷺ exceeded all limits, he was warned about Divine punishment for his misdeeds. He retaliated: "If his message is true, how is it so that I am blessed with such abundance of wealth and children. I would offer all of these as ransom for escaping punishment."

His wife, Umm Jamīl was equally hostile to the Prophet ﷺ. Abū Lahab's enmity was fuelled by her. In the present *Sūrah* both of them

2.	His wealth and what he earned	مَآ أَغْنَىٰ عَنْهُ مَالُهُۥ
	Did not avail him.[2]	وَمَا كَسَبَ ۝
3.	He will soon roast in the Blazing Fire.[3]	سَيَصْلَىٰ نَارًا ذَاتَ لَهَبٍ ۝

are warned against their terrible end. Whoever opposes Truth, be he male or female, related to the Prophet ﷺ or not, great or small, will eventually be humiliated and punished for their opposition to Truth. Kinship with the Prophet ﷺ will not avail anyone. It was pointless on Abū Lahab's part to display such hostile gestures against the Prophet ﷺ and to persecute him. He should better have realised that all his efforts would come to naught. His exalted position was about to end. All his deeds had gone to waste and he was on the verge of utter loss and destruction. This is a Makkan *Sūrah*. It is reported that Abū Lahab was afflicted with smallpox a week after the Battle of Badr. Since it was a contagious disease, his family members drove him out of the house. He died alone and for three days his corpse lay in a highly decomposed state. As its stench became intolerable, labour was hired to clear it away. They dug a grave and pushed the body in with the help of sticks and covered it with stones. It points to his humiliation in this world. As is mentioned in verse 26 of *Sūrah az-Zumar* such unbelievers are destined for a greater punishment in the Hereafter.

2 – His wealth, children, position and glory could not defend him against his punishment.

3 – Soon after his death, he would be consigned to Hellfire. The Qur'ān, therefore, retains his appellation "Abū Lahab". He was known so in that he bore red hot cheeks which shone like flame. However, the Qur'ān clarifies that in terms of his ultimate end he is associated with fire.

4. And his wife who carries the wood.[4]	وَٱمْرَأَتُهُۥ حَمَّالَةَ ٱلْحَطَبِ ﴿٤﴾
5. There is a rope of palm fibres round her neck.[5]	فِى جِيدِهَا حَبْلٌ مِّن مَّسَدٍ ﴿٥﴾

4 – Although Abū Lahab's wife Umm Jamīl was wealthy, she was miserly to the extreme. Every morning she would go to the woods to collect fuel. She spread thorns along the Prophet's way in order to torment him. The Qur'ān clarifies that she was an accomplice of her husband in the persecution of the Prophet ﷺ and in opposition of the Truth. She would accompany her husband in Hell on account of these crimes. She might carry the thorny shrubs – *Zaqqūm* and *Ḍarīʿ* – in Hell. These would serve as the fuel for roasting her husband in Hell. This point is made by Ibn al-Athīr. According to some scholars the expression used for her refers to her bearing tales.

5 – Reference is to a hard rope. For most Qur'ānic scholars, the expression alludes to the fetters in Hell. Furthermore, this expression is in line with the one employed in verse 4 of this *Sūrah*. As it is, one needs a rope to carry wood. It is also said that Umm Jamīl wore a precious necklace. She used to say that she would invest the same in her project to oppose the Prophet ﷺ. While saying so she invoked Lāt and 'Uzzā. It is, therefore, said that a fetter would be around her neck in Hell. It is a significant coincidence that this wretched woman died as the rope was tied to her neck and she suffocated to death.

***

Al-Ikhlāṣ	سُوْرَةُ الْاِخْلَاصِ	The Unity

In the name of Allah, Most Compassionate, Most Merciful.	بِسْمِ اللهِ الرَّحْمٰنِ الرَّحِيْمِ
1. Say: He is Allah, the One.[1]	قُلْ هُوَ اللهُ أَحَدٌ ۝
2. Allah Who is Independent.[2]	اللهُ الصَّمَدُ ۝
3. He does not beget. Nor was He begotten by any.[3]	لَمْ يَلِدْ وَلَمْ يُوْلَدْ ۝

1 – The Prophet ﷺ is directed to tell people who enquired about the nature of Allah, that He is One, without any multiplicity or partner. There is no one equal or similar to Him. This thus refutes Zoroastrian belief that there are two creators – the Yazdān of good and the Ahirman of evil. Likewise, it rejects the Hindu notions of millions of gods and goddesses as partners with Him.

2 – The expression aṣ-Ṣamad has been variously interpreted. While citing all definitions, Ṭabarānī says: "All the interpretations are equally valid in that these represent the numerous attributes of Allah, to Him everyone turns in the hour of crisis. Everyone is dependent upon Him while He does not stand in need of anyone. He represents the perfection of excellence in every respect. He does not need food or drink or anything. He will survive while all creatures will perish." This refutes the notion held by the ignorant ones that others enjoy the same authority as Allah. Furthermore, it denies the Aryan belief about matter and the soul. For them, Allah drew upon both for creation whereas matter and soul are independent of Him. May Allah protect us against entertaining any such notion. Āmeen.

3 – He is not someone's child. Nor does He have any child. This verse strikes at the root of such fallacious notions as mistaking Ezra

4. And there is none equal to Him.[4]	وَلَمْ يَكُن لَّهُۥ كُفُوًا أَحَدٌۢ ۝

and Jesus as sons of God. It states also that no human being should be elevated to Godhead. Moreover, the verse refutes the belief of the polytheists that the angels represented Allah's daughters. The Prophet Jesus عليه السلام was given birth to by a devout woman. Given this, he cannot be looked upon as God either.

4 – Since Allah does not have a peer, He cannot betake a wife or son. The verse refutes the unsound belief of many communities who ascribe others as partners to Him. Some communities went very far in error in identifying Divine Attributes to others. In the religious books of the Jews, one comes across a scene in which the Prophet Jacob عليه السلام has a wrestling bout with Him and even defeats Him. May Allah forbid us. This point is mentioned in verse 5 of *Sūrah al-Kahf* as well.

O Allah! The One True, Unique God, Who does not beget and is not begotten and Who does not have anyone equal to Him! I seek from You my forgiveness. Surely, only You are the Most Forgiving, Most Merciful. *Āmeen.*

***

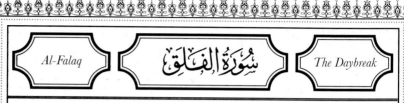

Al-Falaq سُوۡرَةُ الۡفَلَقِ The Daybreak

In the name of Allah, Most
Compassionate, Most Merciful.

1. Say: I seek refuge
with the Lord of the daybreak.[1]

قُلۡ أَعُوذُ بِرَبِّ ٱلۡفَلَقِ ١

2. Against the mischief
of all that He has created.[2]

مِن شَرِّ مَا خَلَقَ ٢

3. And against the evil of the
darkness when it overwhelms.[3]

وَمِن شَرِّ غَاسِقٍ إِذَا وَقَبَ ٣

4. And against the evil

Of women
who tie knots.[4]

ٱلنَّفَّـٰثَـٰتِ فِي ٱلۡعُقَدِ ٤

1 – It is Allah Who brings about the light out of the darkness of
night.

2 – Refuge is sought against the evil of every created being. Some
specific examples follow in this *Sūrah*.

3 – The darkness of night in that most evils, especially magic, are
conducted at night. The reference may be to the lunar eclipse or
the sunset. Shāh 'Abdul Qādir points out that this verse makes
reference to darkness of all sorts, both outward and inward, and
such darkness which is born of error.

4 – This is an allusion to such women or groups or individuals who
tie knots while practising magic. The magic perpetrated against the
Prophet ﷺ by Labeed, a hypocrite was done with the collusion of
some girls. And Allah knows best.

5. And against the evil of the
   malicious one when he envies.[5]   وَمِن شَرِّ حَاسِدٍ إِذَا حَسَدَ ۝

5 – Shāh ʿAbdul Qādir observes: "The evil eye has its spell. And it is a fact." Nonetheless, most Qurʾānic scholars tend to interpret this in a broad sense. When a jealous person cannot control his feelings and demonstrates his jealousy, one should seek shelter against his evil. However, if one feels jealous on the spur of the moment, yet controls oneself, one is not included in the category of people under discussion in this verse.

Let it be clear that jealousy in the present context implies desire on one's part that a divine bounty enjoyed by someone may come to an end. As to feelings of envy, coveting what someone else has, this does not fall into this category. Such a feeling is known as *al-Ghibṭa*. The same point is made in the *Ḥadīth* recorded by Bukhārī: "No (one should) envy except in two cases, the first is a person, whom Allah has given wealth so he spends it righteously, (the second is) one whom Allah has given wisdom and he acts according to it and teaches it to others" the word *ḥasad* (tr. envy) is used in the meaning of *Ghibṭa*.

* * *

| An-Nās | سُورَةُ النَّاس | Mankind |

In the name of Allah, Most Compassionate, Most Merciful.

بِسْمِ اللَّهِ الرَّحْمَٰنِ الرَّحِيمِ

1. Say: I seek refuge with the Lord of mankind.

قُلْ أَعُوذُ بِرَبِّ النَّاسِ ۝

2. King of mankind.

مَلِكِ النَّاسِ ۝

3. God of mankind.[1]

إِلَٰهِ النَّاسِ ۝

4. Against the evil of the whispering one and the hiding one.[2]

مِن شَرِّ الْوَسْوَاسِ الْخَنَّاسِ ۝

5. He who whispers

الَّذِي يُوَسْوِسُ

In the breasts of mankind.

فِي صُدُورِ النَّاسِ ۝

6. From among the *Jinn* and of mankind.[3]

مِنَ الْجِنَّةِ وَالنَّاسِ ۝

---

1 – Although Divine Attributes of Lordship and Rulership are shared in some degree by other creatures, these appear at their sharpest in man. The verse, therefore, makes special mention that Allah is the Lord and Ruler of mankind. Moreover, of all creatures only man suffers from false promptings and doubts.

2 – Even while Satan is invisible, he deceives man. As long as one is lost in negligence, Satan holds complete sway over one. However, as one remembers Allah, Satan vanishes into thin air.

3 – Satans are among both the *Jinn* and among men, and this is also stated in *Sūrah al-An'ām*: "*Likewise did We make for every Messenger an*

enemy, – *satans among men and Jinns, inspiring each other with flowery discourses of deception*" [6: 112]. May Allah protect us against the devils from among both men and *Jinn*.

It is reported on the authority of some Companions, as for example, 'Ā'ishāh, Ibn 'Abbās, and Zayd ibn Arqam, may Allah be pleased with them all, that the Jews subjected the Prophet ﷺ to a magic spell. The whole body of the Prophet ﷺ was affected by a kind of malady. He would, for example, do something and then forget that he had done it. It is worth clarifying that this only happened in relation to his mundane activities, it did not afflict his Prophetic duties in any way. Likewise, he sometimes thought that he had done something which he had not actually performed. As a remedy, Allah sent down these two *Sūrahs* - *al-Falaq* and *an-Nās*. Thanks to their effect, the Prophet ﷺ recovered completely by Allah's leave. Let us be clear that the above report about the magic spell cast upon the Prophet ﷺ is recorded in Bukhārī's and Muslim's collection of *Ḥadīth*. These reports are not contested up to this day by any *Ḥadīth* scholar.

Magic in relation to the Prophet ﷺ does not reflect upon his exalted status. It is on record that the Prophet ﷺ sometimes fell ill and at other times he fainted. At times, he committed some minor lapse while praying. On all these occasions, the Prophet ﷺ made it a point to tell the Companions that he was a mortal human being like them, subject to forgetfulness, like any other fellow human being is. He asked them to remind him if he forgot something. On coming to know of these reports about his illness, fainting and forgetfulness, one might hold that it is hard to believe in him or in the Revelation sent down to him. For he might have committed some lapse with regard to Revelation as well. That the Prophet ﷺ was subject to committing lapses or forgetfulness does not necessarily mean that one should entertain doubts about his Prophetic role and the Revelation sent down to him. If he occasionally suffered from forgetfulness, it should not lead one to disbelieve in his Prophetic role. For such lapses as forgetfulness, illness and fainting are common to all human beings. Since Messengers are human beings, these lapses do not reflect adversely on their exalted position. Since it is borne out by incontestable argument and evidence that he was a true Messenger of Allah, whose infallibility has been ensured by Allah and Who has promised an error-free arrangement for the communication of Divine Revelation through him, it is impossible that any power on earth may obstruct the Prophet 🙵 from performing his Prophetic role. The unbelievers rejected the Messengers as those under the spell of magic in the sense that they disbelieved in them. They thought that they did not act on reason in preaching faith. For them, they were mad or bewitched people. Accordingly, they dismissed Revelation as the ravings of a mad person. May Allah protect us against entertaining such false and outrageous notions. The Qur'ān makes a point of refuting these baseless charges. Nonetheless the Qur'ān never claims that the Messengers transcend humanness. Nor does the Qur'ān rule out the effect of magic upon them. For the spell upon the Prophet 🙵 did not prevent him from performing his Prophetic role.

Note: Many Qur'ānic scholars have presented a large body of insightful points about the last two *Sūrahs* – *al-Falaq* and *an-Nās*. It is not possible to recount in this work the views expressed by Ḥāfiẓ Ibn Qayyim, Imām Rāzī, Ibn Sīnā and Shāh 'Abdul 'Azīz Muḥaddith Dehlawī. Let us recount only Maulānā Muḥammad Qāsim Nanotawī's comment, which should serve as a fitting conclusion to this work:

This is the observable law of nature that as a plant makes its appearance, the gardener exerts himself in looking after it. Until the plant gains full strength and maturity, it has to be tended carefully. Now let us think of the forces which are inimical to the growth and survival of the plant or which deprive the master of reaping the fruits of the plant. It is against these hostile forces that the gardener takes his position. On a little reflection, it appears that such calamities befall us in four ways and accordingly the gardener has to take four measures to fight against these calamities:

i) The plant is to be protected against animals and vermin, lest they eat or destroy it. This protection is especially to be taken against herbivorous animals.

ii) The plant should be supplied with a constant supply of water and heat, especially in terms of sunlight which may help the plant attain its natural growth.

iii) Measures are to be taken to protect the plant against hailstorm, frost, etc. which might strike a fatal blow. These might also stunt its growth.

iv) It is to be seen that someone does not destroy the plant by uprooting it out of jealousy towards the master of the plant. If the gardener takes measures to cover the above four possibilities, he may look forward to Divine Mercy for the growth and maturity of the plant. It is likely that such a plant will yield fruits and that it will benefit many creatures.

By the same analogy, Allah is the Creator of the heavens and the earth, He is the Lord of the morning and causes the birth of everything. He is the Gardener and Protector of the whole universe. Let us seek protection for our Faith and our existence in the same manner, as is stated with respect to defending and protecting a plant against the four types of calamities. We learn that as destroying and devouring plants is in the nature of animals, verse 2 of *Sūrah al-Falaq* refers to the evil innate in all creatures. Such evil is part of their nature, as is evident from their behaviour, for example, in the scorpion and other beasts.

Verse 3 of this *Sūrah* directs that Allah's refuge be sought against the darkness of the night or after sunset or lunar eclipse. The evil referred to here is the one which appears after sunset. Or it signifies when something withdraws and it is no longer possible to draw upon it freely. This applies to the whole chain of cause and effect in the universe. Without known cause and effect man cannot proceed. We have covered this point in our above discussion on how to protect the plant in asserting that arrangements be made to provide the plant with all that is essential to its life such as water, air and sunlight.

Another thing against which Allah's refuge is to be sought is magic. Those who believe in magic recognise that under the spell of magic one loses one's natural abilities. Taken in this sense, magic resembles hailstorm or frost in the above analogy in that both cause the loss of natural growth. It emerges from reports that a hypocrite by the name of Labeed ibn A'ṣam had clouded the Prophet's natural behaviour. This state was, however, over as Gabriel, with Allah's leave, removed the magic spell.

The last danger is jealousy. As we mentioned in the above analogy, an enemy of the gardener might uproot the plant out of jealousy. The issue of jealousy is eloquently stated in verse 5 of this *Sūrah*. It is nonetheless likely that a plant may not enjoy its natural growth in that before its appearance, it might be eaten away by insects, rendering the seed unable to sprout. This point is covered in *Sūrah an-Nās* in the directive to seek protection against the promptings of devils. It also covers the doubts and suspicions which weaken Faith from within. Allah alone can help one defend against these. Since Faith can counter doubts, it is suggested that such measures be taken which may strengthen Faith. It is common knowledge that Faith is reinforced by witnessing Allah's numerous favours and bounties. On observing His immeasurable Lordship, man recognises that Allah is the absolute Master and Ruler, for it is He Who provides all physical and spiritual sustenance. Only someone as perfect as Allah can ensure this sustenance on such a large scale. For He controls everything and nothing in the universe lies outside His authority. Allah alone is entitled to be taken as the Absolute Master and Ruler. Such attributes befit only Him. This point is also made in verse 16 of *Sūrah al-Mu'min*. The attribute of Mastership is closely related with that of Lordship. For the latter consists in showering bounties and defending one against dangers and losses of all sorts. Only the absolute Master can accomplish these twin roles. Going a step further, one realises that only the absolute Master can be the Lord and object of all worship. By definition, the Lord is One to whom others surrender, while disregarding all others besides Him. It is obvious that submission is deserved only by Allah, for He enjoys total authority and power. Taken in this sense, Allah alone has the attributes of

Lordship and Godhead. It is stated in verse 76 of *Sūrah al-Mā'idah* that the unbelievers worship those who cannot inflict any harm upon them or do them any favour.

The first and the foremost prerequisite of Faith is belief in Lordship, followed by the attributes of Mastership and Divinity. Whoever seeks to defend his Faith against false promptings and doubts should turn to Allah Who is the Lord of Mankind, King of Mankind and God of Mankind, the three Divine Attributes featuring in three verses of *Sūrah an-Nās*. Promptings are contrasted with attributes of Divinity, for Allah alone can grant refuge to mankind. That He is the absolute Master and Lord helps one gain access to Him. These Divine attributes are contrasted with *al-Khannās*. Implicit in the expression are the promptings infused by Satan when man is in a state of negligence. As one gains Faith and overcomes one's doubts, Satan makes a hasty retreat. It is the bounden duty of the Master to defend his subjects against the wicked and their oppression. Accordingly, Allah is spoken of as the King or Master of Mankind, which contrasts with the expression *al-Khannās*. Since *al-Khannās* cause false promptings in people's hearts, they are akin to thieves who break in. It is obvious that the Divine attributes mentioned in this *Sūrah* have a fitting correspondence with the evils against which refuge is sought.

* * *

| Al-Fātiḥah | سُوْرَةُ الْفَاتِحَةِ | The Opening Sūrah |

1. (Say, I begin) In the name of Allah Who is Most Compassionate, Most Merciful.[1]   بِسْمِ اللَّهِ الرَّحْمَٰنِ الرَّحِيمِ ﴿١﴾

2. All praises are for Allah,[2] Who is the Lord of all the Worlds,[3]   الْحَمْدُ لِلَّهِ رَبِّ الْعَالَمِينَ ﴿٢﴾

3. Most Compassionate, Most Merciful.   الرَّحْمَٰنِ الرَّحِيمِ ﴿٣﴾

4. Master of the Day of Recompense.[4]   مَالِكِ يَوْمِ الدِّينِ ﴿٤﴾

1 – Both the Qur'ānic expressions "ar-Raḥmān" and "ar-Raḥīm" are the intense form of the adjective. The former is the superlative degree.

2 – All praises, in their perfection and in the past, present and future, befit Allah ﷻ alone. For He has created and granted every bounty. He grants it directly or indirectly. To use a parable, if one benefits from the sunlight in terms of light and heat, it represents one benefiting from the sun itself.

3 – Included in "al-ʿĀlam" the world, are all types of creation hence al-ʿĀlam is not used in its plural form. In the verse under study the "Worlds" embraces everything ranging from the world of Jinn, of angels and of human beings. Therefore, the expression al-ʿĀlamīn, the worlds, is used in its plural form in order to bring out the fact that everyone is the creation of Allah, the Supreme Lord.

4 – Its special mention is owing to the fact that great events will happen on this Day. This Day will be unique in terms of its dreadfulness. No one other than Allah ﷻ, the True One will exercise authority on that Day. It is stated elsewhere in the Qur'ān that the dominion will belong wholly to Allah ﷻ on the Day of Judgement.

5. Only You we worship and only from You we seek help.[5]	إِيَّاكَ نَعْبُدُ وَإِيَّاكَ نَسْتَعِينُ ۝
6. Guide us to the straight way.	اَهْدِنَا الصِّرَاطَ الْمُسْتَقِيمَ ۝
7. The way of those who have been blessed by You,[6]	صِرَاطَ الَّذِينَ أَنْعَمْتَ عَلَيْهِمْ
Not those who incurred Your wrath	غَيْرِ الْمَغْضُوبِ عَلَيْهِمْ
And not of those who went astray.[7]	وَلَا الضَّآلِّينَ ۝

5 – It emerges from the verse that it is unlawful to invoke help from anyone other than Allah.

6 – As to those blessed by Allah, they are: "Messengers, the truthful, the martyrs and the righteous." This point is fully brought out at other places in the Qur'ān. *"those who incurred Your wrath"* refers to the Jews whereas *"those who went astray"* stands for the Christians. One learns from other Qur'ānic verses and authentic *Aḥādīth* that one goes astray from the straight way in either of the two ways. First, it might be because of the lack of knowledge. Or it might be a deliberate act of going astray. Christians belong to the former category and Jews to the latter.

7 – This *Sūrah* is by way of the supplication made by man. Allah instructs man how to supplicate to Him when seeking His help. It is part of the *Sunnah* to conclude the recitation of the *Sūrah* with uttering *"Āmeen"*, though this expression does not figure in the Qur'ān itself. Literally, it means "so be it". The intended meaning is that man prays that he should follow the righteous ones and be distinct from the rebels and disobedient ones. The first half of the *Sūrah* is devoted to the praise of Allah while the second half constitutes man's supplication.

* * *

INDEX

152